30-Minute Italian

30-Minute Italian

Fran Warde

Photography by David Loftus

Bounty
Books

Part of the **MYRiAD** series

First published in Great Britain in 1998 by Hamlyn,
a division of Octopus Publishing Group Ltd
Revised editions published 2004, 2008

This edition published in 2011 by Bounty Books,
a division of Octopus Publishing Group Ltd,
Endeavour House, 189 Shaftesbury Avenue,
London WC2H 8JY
www.octopusbooks.co.uk

An Hachette UK Company
www.hachette.co.uk

Fran Warde asserts the moral right to be identified
as the author of this work

ISBN 978-0-753721-67-4

A CIP catalogue record for this book is available
from the British Library

Printed and bound in China

NOTES

1 The Department of Health advises that eggs
should not be consumed raw. It is prudent for
more vulnerable people such as pregnant and
nursing mothers, invalids, the elderly, babies
and young children to avoid uncooked or lightly
cooked dishes made with eggs.

2 Meat and poultry should be cooked
thoroughly. To test if poultry is cooked, pierce
the flesh through the thickest part with a
skewer or fork – the juices should run clear,
never pink or red.

3 This book includes dishes made with nuts
and nut derivatives. It is advisable for those
with known allergic reactions to nuts and nut
derivatives and those who may be potentially
vulnerable to these allergies, such as pregnant
and nursing mothers, invalids, the elderly,
babies and children, to avoid dishes made with
nuts and nut oils. It is also prudent to check the
labels of pre-prepared ingredients for the
possible inclusion of nut derivatives.

contents

introduction 7

glossary 9

soups 12

pasta 22

risotto 38

pizza and polenta 48

salads 60

vegetables 72

fish and shellfish 86

poultry, game and meat 98

desserts 114

index 126

introduction

Cooking for me started at a very young age when I would help my mum in the kitchen (I'm not sure if it was help, but it was always great fun), spilling sugar and flour everywhere and seeing who could mix the fastest! As soon as she taught me that part of cooking was also clearing up, I was allowed to cook more and more – cakes on Saturday afternoon, then, later, fish pies and lasagne. I went to a boarding school with dreadful food, but on Tuesdays it was domestic science; I would try to make a decent meal for a few friends to enjoy. Everyone relied on it working out, which it generally did.

I think that these early days played a great part in creating the foundations for my cooking career. I still enjoy it and continue to learn; it's a never-ending creative process of combining colours, flavours and textures to produce a delicious meal to enjoy with friends.

I have aimed to produce imaginative and tasty recipes that are quick and simple to make (and good for you, too). The recipes in this book have been designed to show that it's possible to produce delicious, mouthwatering meals in 30 minutes – the same length of time that it takes to heat up many ready-made meals – or even less time, without resorting to convenience food.

Italian recipes fit the bill perfectly when you need good, quick meals in a hurry, for the Italians are very keen on fresh food and speedy methods of preparation. They take their food very seriously, combining a deep respect for top-quality ingredients with a great love of home cooking – in fact, the way to enjoy Italian food at its best is to eat in people's homes.

Italian food, in all its rich, regional diversity, doesn't just taste delicious – it's actually good for you, too. The Mediterranean diet, with its emphasis on fresh vegetables and fruit, fresh fish and seafood, pasta and olive oil, is reckoned to be one of the healthiest in the world, full of vitamins and minerals and low in saturated fat.

In this book I have included a lot of vegetable recipes, which work very well as supper dishes on their own. Serve two or three vegetable, pasta or rice dishes together, enjoy their delicate flavours and see how satisfied you are after the meal without feeling at all heavy or as if you have eaten too much. There are some delicious meat and fish recipes, too, which can be cooked in 30 minutes – a joy to any busy cook who doesn't want to be chained to the stove when the sun is shining outside or after a busy day at work or with the children. There are also some puddings for those special days.

I have to say that I am especially proud of the chocolate risotto, which is a totally new idea and easy to make from ingredients that can be found in any well-stocked kitchen.

Do follow the Italian example and shop carefully, though. Some of the cheaper products in our shops and supermarkets are very poor substitutes for the real thing. Never, for example, buy ready-grated Parmesan cheese; instead, buy a piece and grate it as required. A guide to the most important or unusual ingredients used in the recipes appears in the glossary that follows.

Fran Warde

glossary

balsamic vinegar This aristocrat of vinegars is made in Modena. The grape juice is aged in wooden barrels for an average of seven years. Like a good wine, balsamic vinegar needs time to mature, and the longer it is in the barrel, the deeper and sweeter the flavour.

capers Used to flavour sauces, these are the pungent, sharp-tasting buds of a shrub found in Mediterranean countries. Capers are usually bottled in brine and need to be rinsed in water before using. Small ones are the best.

cavolo nero A long, slim cabbage with a distinct sweet flavour; it is a beautiful green with a hint of purplish black.

cheeses

Dolcelatte A soft, creamy cows' milk cheese with blue veins, aged for two months; it is similar to Gorgonzola but milder.
Fontina A soft cows' milk cheese from the Val d'Aosta in the Italian Alps, which is aged for up to five months. It is reminiscent of Gruyère and used in cooking and as a dessert cheese.
Mascarpone A soft, creamy cheese made with cows' milk and used for both sweet and savoury dishes.
Mozzarella Originally made from buffaloes' milk, it is now more often made from cows' milk or a mixture of the two. Cows' milk mozzarella does not have the same softness of flavour. Mozzarella should be eaten fresh; it melts well and is frequently used on pizzas.
Parmesan This strong, hard cheese is made from partially skimmed cows' milk and aged for up to two years. The best Parmesan has the words Parmigiano-Reggiano punched into the rind. Buy it in a block and grate it as you need it.
Pecorino This ewes' milk cheese can be soft or hard depending on its age; it is made all over Italy, so flavours can vary greatly. Mature, hard pecorino is used for grating like Parmesan.
Ricotta A bland, soft, fresh cheese used as a base in fillings and frequently combined with spinach. It should be used when it is very fresh.

chocolate Bars of chocolate vary so much in their cocoa content. Look on the back of the packet and only use ones that contain at least 70% cocoa solids. I prefer Valrhona which can be found in good delicatessens.

ciabatta A popular Italian bread baked into a flat loaf with a distinctive open texture. It can have a range of flavourings added.

fennel A beautiful, fragrant vegetable with a delicate aniseed flavour, fennel is wonderful with fish; use the feathery fronds to add to salsa verde.

focaccia A flat yeast bread made with olive oil and baked in an oiled pan. It is often flavoured with garlic, herbs, sun-dried tomatoes or olives.

garlic A pungent herb used extensively in Italian cooking. Crush heavily with the side of a knife to remove the papery skin, then the clove can be chopped.

herbs

Basil The best-known Italian herb with soft, bright green leaves, basil is a vital ingredient in pesto and goes well with tomatoes. There is also a red basil with small, purplish leaves and a more delicate flavour.

Bay leaves Usually used dried in soups and stews as part of a bouquet garni.

Oregano A sweet, spicy and aromatic herb, similar to marjoram.

Rosemary Its long, spiky leaves give rosemary a distinctive appearance. It is used a great deal in Italy, particularly with chicken and lamb. Rosemary is very pungent, so should be used in moderation.

olive oil

Extra virgin olive oil, virgin olive oil and olive oil. These names refer to the way that the oil is extracted and this can greatly alter the flavour. Try to buy extra virgin oil from the first cold pressing as this will be rich in flavour and is most suitable for dressings, sauces and pouring over pasta. A less expensive oil can be used for frying.

olives

Small, oval tree fruits which ripen from green to black. For the best flavour, buy them from delicatessens that sell them loose rather than in bottles or cans.

pancetta

The same cut as streaky bacon but differently cured, pancetta is found in supermarkets or in delicatessens. It is also sold as pancetta arrotolata, in a roll like salami. Buy a 1 cm/½ inch slice, unroll it and use as pancetta.

panettone

A baked yeast cake from Milan enriched with egg yolks, raisins and candied peel. Panettone is traditionally served at Christmas or with coffee; it is very good toasted at breakfast.

parma ham

A great Italian delicacy, this cured ham comes from the area around Parma in the Emilia-Romagna region of northern Italy. The skin is rubbed in salt, then the hams are hung in cellars to mature for 8–10 months. Parma ham must be served thinly sliced; it is eaten on its own or with melon or fresh figs.

pasta

This is made from hard durum wheat flour and water. If it is made with eggs, it is called *pasta all'ouvo*. I prefer fresh pasta but a good dried Italian brand can be substituted. The Italians do not usually eat pasta as a main course, but serve a light pasta dish between the antipasti and the main course. It is available in a bewildering range of shapes and sizes.

pasta shapes

Farfalle or **farfallini** Pasta bows.

Fusilli Pasta twists or corkscrews.

Lasagne Large sheets of pasta used for baked dishes. Sheets can be cut to fit cooking dishes.

Linguine Long, thin, flat ribbon noodles.

Pappardelle Wide pasta noodles.

Penne Sometimes known as quills, these are short, tubular lengths of pasta.

Orecchiette Small, round, ear-shaped pasta.

Orzo A very small pasta shape, which looks rather like grains of rice.

Spaghetti Long, string-like pasta.

Tagliatelle Long, flat ribbon noodles.

Tortellini Pasta twists with various fillings.

pine nuts Small, slim, soft nuts with an oily texture, these come from the Mediterranean stone pine tree. Pine nuts, also known as pine kernels, are used in pasta sauces, stuffings and salads and are usually browned before using. They turn rancid quickly, so store them in a refrigerator.

polenta Ground maize (corn) kernels mixed with water, made into a flat, golden loaf, sliced and grilled. Polenta needs to be flavoured as it is bland, although it is rich in vitamins. It can also be served in a softer form, like mashed potatoes.

pumpkin seed oil Pressed from roasted pumpkin seeds, this thick, brown oil, tinged with green, has a wonderfully powerful, toasted flavour.

puy lentils Small, round lentils, greenish brown in colour and far superior to any other lentil for texture and flavour. They come from the area around Le Puy in France.

risotto rice Arborio is the classic risotto rice from Piedmont. It absorbs a lot of cooking liquid without becoming too soft. The grain is plump and irregular, translucent at the edges with a hard, white core. It produces a creamy risotto with a slight bite. Carnaroli is very similar.

saffron The dried stigmas of a species of crocus, with a pungent aroma, bitter flavour and a beautiful golden colour. Buy it in Spain or at duty-free shops where it is cheaper and comes in larger containers.

sea salt I think Maldon sea salt from Essex is by far the best; there are no additives and the large, flaky crystals are fantastic on a salad or used at the table.

squashes These are members of the marrow and pumpkin family; the best is butternut squash for its sweet flavour and dense texture.

sun-dried tomatoes Intensely flavoured dried tomatoes that add zip to a dish. Those bottled in oil are more convenient to use than the dried variety, which need to be soaked before use.

truffle oil The infusion of truffle juices into an oil, usually extra virgin olive oil. White truffle oil is usually more expensive and stronger in flavour than black truffle oil. Use both sparingly as they have an intense flavour.

wild mushrooms

Chanterelles Wonderful aromatic mushrooms with a perfumed taste, chanterelles are shaped like open horns, torn around the edges. They vary in colour from brown to gold and dry well.

Morels Mushrooms with bulbous pitted caps and an intense aroma. Fresh morels need to be cleaned well. They are also found in dried and bottled forms.

Porcini Delicious mushrooms with a deep, rich flavour, porcini have a round, bun-like cap, a thick chubby stalk and fleshy texture. They are sold fresh and dried. Soak dried porcini in hot water for 15 minutes before use, then drain, filter and reserve the water to use as a rich stock.

Truffles The mysterious king of fungi, these are found below ground near oak trees and are sniffed out by pigs or dogs in autumn and winter. Usually the size of a walnut, truffles are rough on the outside, dense inside and firm to the touch. Both white and black truffles are found; their flavour is so intense that only a little is needed. Truffles are best served raw, finely shaved over salad or pasta.

soups

In Italy, soup is served as a *primo piatto*, first course, as an alternative to rice or pasta. Many of the soups are hearty, based on beans, vegetables and bread, and thus make complete meals in themselves.

spinach and broccoli soup

preparation time **10 mins**
cooking time **20 mins**
total time **30 mins** serves **4**

2 tablespoons olive oil
50 g/2 oz butter
1 onion, diced
1 garlic clove, crushed
2 potatoes, chopped
250 g/8 oz broccoli, chopped
300 g/10 oz spinach, chopped
900 ml/1½ pints chicken or vegetable stock
125 g/4 oz Gorgonzola cheese, crumbled
   into small pieces
juice of ½ lemon
½ teaspoon grated nutmeg
salt and pepper
75 g/3 oz toasted pine nuts, to garnish
warm crusty bread, to serve

one Heat the oil and butter in a saucepan,
add the onion and garlic and sauté for
3 mins.
two Add the chopped potatoes, broccoli,
spinach and stock, bring to the boil and
simmer for 15 mins.
three This soup can be puréed or left with
chunky pieces. Add the Gorgonzola to the
soup with the lemon juice, nutmeg and
salt and pepper to taste. Garnish with the
toasted pine nuts and serve with warm
crusty bread.

melon and parma ham soup

preparation time **10 mins**
total time **10 mins** serves **4**

1 ripe cantaloupe or charentais melon,
   weighing about 1.5 kg/3 lb
8 slices of Parma ham
salt and pepper
red basil leaves, torn, to garnish

one Cut the melon in half and remove
the seeds. Scoop the flesh into a food
processor or blender and whizz until
smooth, then add salt and pepper to taste.
two Finely dice 4 of the ham slices and
stir them into the soup. Cut the remaining
4 slices into thin ribbons.
three Garnish the soup with the ham
ribbons and torn basil leaves.

Serve at room temperature or just slightly
chilled. When food is too cold, you
cannot taste its full flavour.

pesto and green vegetable soup

preparation time **10 mins**
cooking time **20 mins**
total time **30 mins** serves **4**

PESTO
3 garlic cloves, crushed
handful of basil leaves
2 tablespoons pine nuts
50 g/2 oz Parmesan cheese, freshly grated
3 tablespoons olive oil

SOUP
3 tablespoons olive oil
1 onion, diced
2 leeks, sliced
1 potato, chopped
425 g/14 oz can haricot beans, drained
   and rinsed
1.5 litres/2½ pints vegetable stock
2 courgettes, diced
125 g/4 oz small green beans, chopped
125 g/4 oz broccoli florets, chopped
250 g/8 oz canned artichoke hearts
1 tablespoon flat leaf parsley, chopped
salt and pepper

one To make the pesto, put the garlic, basil, pine nuts and Parmesan into a food processor or blender and purée thoroughly. Add the oil and blend again. Set aside.
two Heat the oil for the soup in a saucepan, add the onion and leeks and cook over a gentle heat for about 3 mins.
three Add the potato, haricot beans, stock and salt and pepper to taste, bring to the boil and simmer for 12 mins.
four Add the vegetables and simmer for 5 mins. Stir in the parsley and pesto and serve.

minestrone soup

preparation time **5 mins**
cooking time **25 mins**
total time **30 mins** serves **4**

2 tablespoons olive oil
1 onion, diced
1 garlic clove, crushed
2 celery sticks, chopped
1 leek, finely sliced
1 carrot, chopped
400 g/13 oz can chopped tomatoes
600 ml/1 pint chicken or vegetable stock
1 courgette, diced
½ small cabbage, shredded
1 bay leaf
75 g/3 oz canned haricot beans
75 g/3 oz spaghetti, broken into small pieces
1 tablespoon flat leaf parsley, chopped
salt and pepper

TO SERVE
50 g/2 oz Parmesan cheese, freshly grated
bruschetta (see page 20)

one Heat the oil in a saucepan, add the onion, garlic, celery, leek and carrot and sauté for 3 mins.
two Add the tomatoes, stock, courgette, cabbage, bay leaf and beans. Bring to the boil and simmer for 10 mins.
three Add the broken spaghetti and season with salt and pepper to taste. Stir well and cook for a further 8 mins. Keep stirring as the soup may stick to the bottom of the pan.
four Just before serving, add the chopped parsley and stir well. Serve with grated Parmesan and bruschetta.

butternut squash soup

preparation time **5 mins**
cooking time **25 mins**
total time **30 mins** serves **4**

1 butternut squash, weighing 875 g/1¾ lb
50 g/2 oz butter
2 tablespoons olive oil
2 onions, chopped
1 garlic clove, crushed
1 litre/1¾ pints chicken or vegetable stock
pinch of saffron threads
salt and pepper

TO SERVE
2 rosemary sprigs, chopped
75 g/3 oz Parmesan cheese, freshly grated

one To prepare the squash, cut it in half
and remove all the seeds, peel off the skin
and chop the flesh into small dice.
two Heat the butter and oil in a saucepan,
add the onions, garlic and squash and sauté
for 5 mins.
three Add the stock and saffron, bring to
the boil and simmer for 15 mins.
four Pour the soup into a food processor
or blender and work to a purée. Season
generously with salt and pepper.
five To serve, ladle into warmed bowls and
sprinkle each one with chopped rosemary
and a generous spoonful of grated Parmesan.

Like Minestrone, Tuscan bean soup can be reheated and, as it improves with keeping, it is really worth making the day before and storing in the refrigerator, allowing all the flavours to mingle.

mussel soup

preparation time **10 mins**
cooking time **10 mins**
total time **20 mins** serves **4**

2 tablespoons olive oil
2 onions, chopped
2 garlic cloves, crushed
1 red chilli, deseeded and chopped
150 g/5 oz piece of green bacon, chopped
1 kg/2 lb mussels, scrubbed and debearded
2 x 400 g/13 oz cans chopped tomatoes
½ bottle dry white wine
good pinch of saffron threads
handful of flat leaf parsley, roughly chopped
salt and pepper

one Warm the oil in a large saucepan.
Add the onions, garlic, chilli and bacon
and sauté for 5 mins.
two Check the mussels carefully. Discard
any that are open or do not close immediately
when tapped on a work surface.
three Add the mussels, tomatoes, wine,
saffron and salt and pepper to taste and mix
well. Place a tight-fitting lid on the pan and
simmer for 5 mins or until all the mussel
shells have opened. Discard any mussels
with shells that remain shut.
four Add the parsley, stir well and serve
at once.

tuscan bean soup

preparation time **5 mins**
cooking time **25 mins**
total time **30 mins** serves **4**

2 tablespoons olive oil
4 shallots, chopped
2 garlic cloves, crushed
150 g/5 oz piece of green bacon, diced
1 carrot, diced
2 celery sticks, diced
½ red pepper, cored, deseeded and diced
425 g/14 oz can borlotti beans, drained and
   rinsed
1 litre/1¾ pints chicken stock
1 bay leaf
1 teaspoon chopped oregano
1 teaspoon chopped marjoram
handful of flat leaf parsley, chopped
salt and pepper
extra virgin olive oil, to drizzle

one Heat the olive oil in a saucepan, add the
shallots, garlic, bacon, carrot, celery and red
pepper and cook, stirring occasionally, for
5 mins.
two Add the beans, stock, bay leaf, oregano
and marjoram, bring to the boil and simmer
for 15 mins. Skim off any scum that may
come from the beans.
three Taste and season well. Finally, just
before serving, add the chopped parsley.
four To serve, ladle into warmed bowls
and drizzle each one with a little extra virgin
olive oil.

bruschetta

preparation time **5 mins**
cooking time **5 mins**
total time **10 mins** serves **4**

8 slices of ciabatta bread
2 garlic cloves, peeled
small handful of flat leaf parsley, chopped
5 tablespoons olive oil
salt

one Toast the bread under a preheated grill
until golden brown.
two Rub the garlic over one side of the
bread; the bread acts as a grater and the
garlic is evenly spread over the bread.
Sprinkle the bruschetta with the parsley
and salt to taste and drizzle with the oil.
Serve immediately or keep warm until
required, but do not keep warm for too long
or the bruschetta will lose its crunchiness.

Bruschetta is delicious served with many
different Italian dishes, especially soup and
fish. It is a very useful accompaniment as
the bread does not have to be fresh.

crostini

preparation time **10 mins**
cooking time **5 mins**
total time **15 mins** serves **4**

8 slices of ciabatta bread
2 garlic cloves, peeled
small handful of flat leaf parsley, chopped
5 tablespoons olive oil
1–2 red peppers, cored, deseeded, skinned
    and sliced into strips (see page 35)
75 g/3 oz black olives, pitted
125 g/4 oz goats' cheese, crumbled
salt and pepper

one Toast the bread under a preheated grill
until golden brown.
two Rub the garlic over one side of the
bread; the bread acts as a grater and the
garlic is evenly spread over the bread.
Sprinkle with the parsley and salt to taste
and drizzle with the oil.
three Mix together the red peppers, olives
and crumbled goats' cheese and season
with pepper.
four Spread the mixture evenly over the
toasted bruschetta and place under a
preheated low grill for 2 mins to just melt
the cheese. Serve at once.

variation Sliced tomatoes, sprinkled with
chopped oregano and pepper, are also very
good on bruschetta.

Crostini are an extension of bruschetta – the base is the
same but the crostini have many different toppings.
They are great with soup; if you want to serve a simple
supper, there is nothing better than a good home-made
soup, crostini with your favourite topping and a fresh
green salad.

pasta

Well over 200 different
shapes of pasta are
available in Italy and
every region has its own
particular specialities and
ways of serving them.
Pasta is one of the most
versatile Italian foods
and may be baked,
stuffed and tossed in
sauces or dressings.

pasta primavera

preparation time **15 mins**
cooking time **15 mins**
total time **30 mins** serves **4**

2 tablespoons olive oil
1 garlic clove, crushed
2 shallots, chopped
125 g/4 oz shelled peas
125 g/4 oz young broad beans, shelled
125 g/4 oz asparagus, trimmed
125 g/4 oz spinach, chopped
300 g/10 oz tagliatelle
150 ml/¼ pint whipping cream
75 g/3 oz Parmesan cheese, freshly grated
handful of mint leaves, chopped
salt and pepper

one Heat the oil in a saucepan, add the
garlic and shallots and sauté for 3 mins. Add
the peas, beans, asparagus and spinach to
the shallot mixture. Stir well and cook for
2 mins.
two Meanwhile, bring a large saucepan of
water to the boil. Cook the tagliatelle for
3 mins if fresh or 7 mins if dried, or
according to packet instructions. Stir the
pasta while it is cooking.
three Stir the cream into the vegetables,
mix well and simmer for 3 mins.
four Drain the tagliatelle thoroughly, then
add the pasta to the vegetable sauce and
season well with salt and pepper. Add the
Parmesan and mint and toss thoroughly with
2 spoons. Serve at once.

linguine with vegetables

preparation time **10 mins**
cooking time **10 mins**
total time **20 mins** serves **4**

1 red pepper, cored, deseeded and chopped
1 courgette, sliced
1 red onion, sliced
1 small aubergine, sliced into thin rounds
8 asparagus spears, trimmed
5 tablespoons olive oil
300 g/10 oz linguine
3 tablespoons frozen petits pois
125 g/4 oz Parmesan cheese, freshly grated
handful of basil leaves, roughly torn
salt and pepper

one Heat a griddle pan. Add the red
pepper, skin side down, and griddle until
the skin blisters and blackens. Griddle the
courgette, onion and aubergine slices and
the asparagus for 2 mins on each side.
Alternatively, cook all the vegetables under
a preheated hot grill.
two Peel the skin off the pepper and
slice into ribbons. Place in a dish with
the courgette, onion, aubergine and
asparagus. Drizzle with oil. Keep warm
in a low oven.
three Meanwhile, bring a large saucepan
of water to the boil. Cook the linguine for
3–4 mins if fresh or 8 mins if dried, or
according to packet instructions. Add the
petits pois for the last minute of the
cooking time.
four Drain the pasta and petits pois, then
return to the saucepan. Add the vegetables,
seasoning and Parmesan. Toss well, adding
a little more oil if necessary. Add the basil
and toss again, then serve immediately.

Cooking the vegetables for this dish on a heated
griddle pan or under a preheated hot grill intensifies
their individual flavours.

penne with tomato and chilli

preparation time **10 mins**
cooking time **20 mins**
total time **30 mins** serves **4**

3 tablespoons olive oil
1 onion, chopped
2 garlic cloves, crushed
2 pinches of crushed dried chillies
300 g/10 oz penne
10 plum tomatoes
1 teaspoon sugar
1 teaspoon vinegar
handful of flat leaf parsley, chopped
extra virgin olive oil (optional)
salt and pepper
75 g/3 oz Parmesan cheese, freshly grated,
    to serve

one Heat the olive oil in a saucepan, add the onion and garlic and sauté until soft; do not let them brown. Add the chillies.
two Meanwhile, bring a large saucepan of water to the boil. Cook the penne for 6 mins if fresh or 10 mins if dried, or according to packet instructions.
three Cut a cross at the stem end of each tomato. Place in a heatproof bowl and pour over boiling water to cover. Leave for 1–2 mins, then drain and peel off the skins. Cut the tomatoes into quarters, deseed, then cut lengthways into strips.
four Add the tomatoes to the onion mixture. Over a low heat, add the sugar, vinegar and salt and pepper to taste. Mix gently and simmer slowly until the pasta is cooked.
five Drain the pasta well. Stir the parsley into the tomato sauce. Add the sauce to the pasta. Mix well, adding a dash of extra virgin olive oil, if wished. Serve with Parmesan.

saffron bows

preparation time **5 mins**
cooking time **10 mins**
total time **15 mins** serves **4**

300 g/10 oz farfalle
25 g/1 oz butter
150 ml/¼ pint double cream
½ teaspoon saffron threads
salt and pepper
75 g/3 oz Parmesan cheese, freshly grated,
    to serve

one Bring a large saucepan of water to the boil and cook the farfalle for 3 mins if fresh or 6 mins if dried, or according to packet instructions.
two Heat the butter and cream in a small saucepan, add the saffron and gently bring to a simmer; the yellow of the saffron will explode into the cream and a fantastic subtle aroma will fill the kitchen.
three Drain the pasta well, place in a warmed serving bowl and pour over the saffron sauce. Season with salt and pepper and mix well.
four Serve the Parmesan at the table and sprinkle just a little over each portion.

fusilli with parmesan and pine nuts

preparation time **5 mins**
cooking time **15 mins**
total time **20 mins** serves **4**

300 g/10 oz fusilli
125 g/4 oz pine nuts
75 g/3 oz butter
2 tablespoons olive oil
75 g/3 oz Parmesan cheese, freshly grated
handful of basil leaves
salt and pepper

one Bring a large saucepan of water to the boil and cook the fusilli for 3–4 mins if fresh or 7 mins if dried, or according to packet instructions.
two Toast the pine nuts under a preheated medium grill or in a pan over a moderate heat. Watch them constantly and move them around to brown evenly.
three Melt the butter with the oil in a small saucepan. Drain the pasta well, then pour over the butter, season with salt and pepper and toss well.
four Turn into a warmed serving dish, sprinkle with the pine nuts, Parmesan and basil leaves and serve immediately.

pappardelle with olives and capers

preparation time **10 mins**
cooking time **15 mins**
total time **25 mins** serves **4**

125 g/4 oz black or green olives, pitted
2 pinches of crushed dried chillies
2 tablespoons capers, drained, rinsed and
    chopped
7 anchovy fillets, drained and chopped
4 large pieces sun-dried tomatoes, soaked in
    olive oil
300 g/10 oz pappardelle
large handful of flat leaf parsley, chopped
75 g/3 oz Parmesan cheese, freshly grated
salt and pepper

one Roughly chop the olives. Put them into a saucepan with the chillies, capers and anchovies. Chop the sun-dried tomatoes roughly and add them to the saucepan with 4 tablespoons of the olive oil.
two Gently heat the olive mixture for 4 mins until warm; do not let it fry.
three Meanwhile, bring a large saucepan of boiling water to the boil. Cook the pappardelle for 4 mins if fresh and 7 mins if dried, or according to packet instructions.
four Drain the pasta, then add the warmed olive mixture, parsley and Parmesan. Season with salt and pepper. Mix well with 2 spoons and serve. This dish can also be left to stand for a while and served at room temperature.

This dish is delicious and very good in the summer because of the fresh taste of the lemon and basil. If orzo is not available, another pasta shape can be substituted.

lemon and basil orzo

preparation time **10 mins**
cooking time **10 mins**
total time **20 mins** serves **4**

2 garlic cloves, crushed
large handful of basil leaves
5 tablespoons olive oil
rind and juice of 2 lemons
300 g/10 oz dried orzo
150 g/5 oz Parmesan cheese, freshly grated
salt and pepper

one Using a pestle and mortar or a food processor or blender, blend the garlic, basil, oil and lemon rind and juice together until smooth.
two Meanwhile, bring a large saucepan of water to the boil. Cook the orzo for 6–8 mins, or according to packet instructions.
three Add the Parmesan to the basil mixture, blend well and season with salt and pepper.
four Drain the pasta thoroughly. Add the pesto and mix well so that the sauce is distributed evenly throughout the pasta. Serve immediately.

penne with broad beans, asparagus and mint

preparation time **10 mins**
cooking time **18 mins**
total time **28 mins** serves **4**

500 g/1 lb asparagus, trimmed and cut into
    short lengths
4 tablespoons olive oil
300 g/10 oz penne
250 g/8 oz shelled broad beans or peas
75 ml/3 fl oz double cream
75 g/3 oz Parmesan cheese, freshly grated
4 tablespoons chopped mint
salt and pepper

one Place the asparagus on a baking sheet, brush generously with oil and season with salt and pepper. Place under a preheated grill and cook for 8 mins, turning as they brown.
two Meanwhile, bring a large saucepan of water to the boil and cook the penne for 6 mins if fresh or 10 mins if dried, or according to packet instructions.
three Cook the beans or peas in a separate saucepan of lightly salted boiling water for 2 mins.
four Drain the pasta. Pour the cream into the empty pasta pan over the heat, add the cooked beans or peas, grilled asparagus and Parmesan and season with salt and pepper. Return the cooked pasta to the pan, add the mint and toss well with 2 wooden spoons. Serve at once.

mushroom and mozzarella lasagne stacks

preparation time **10 mins**
cooking time **20 mins**
total time **30 mins** serves **4**

2 tablespoons olive oil
50 g/2 oz butter
2 onions, chopped
2 garlic cloves, crushed
500 g/1 lb mushrooms, sliced
4 tablespoons double cream
4 tablespoons dry white wine
1 teaspoon chopped thyme
8 sheets of fresh lasagne
2 red peppers, cored, deseeded, skinned and
  thickly sliced (see page 35)
125 g/4 oz baby spinach leaves, chopped
125 g/4 oz packet buffalo mozzarella cheese,
  sliced
50 g/2 oz Parmesan cheese shavings
salt and pepper

one Heat the oil and butter in a saucepan, add the onions and sauté for 3 mins. Add the garlic and cook for 1 min.

two Add the mushrooms, turn up the heat and cook for 5 mins.

three Add the cream, wine and thyme, season with salt and pepper and simmer for 4 mins.

four Bring a large saucepan of water to the boil, add the lasagne, a few sheets at a time, checking that it does not stick together, and cook for 3 mins if fresh or 7 mins if dried. Remove and place 4 pieces in a well-oiled, large ovenproof dish.

five Place a generous spoonful of mushroom mixture on each piece of lasagne, add some red pepper slices and half of the spinach leaves and put another piece of lasagne on top. Then add the remaining spinach, a slice of mozzarella and top with a little more mushroom mixture. Finish with some Parmesan shavings. Place the lasagne portions under a preheated very hot grill and cook for 5 mins or until the mushroom mixture is bubbling and the Parmesan is golden.

This dish can be cooked in advance except for the final browning of the Parmesan. Reheat in a moderate oven for 20 mins, then grill until golden.

spaghetti vongole

preparation time **10 mins**
cooking time **20 mins**
total time **30 mins** serves **4**

1.5 kg/3 lb baby clams (vongole)
4 tablespoons olive oil
2 garlic cloves, crushed
125 ml/4 fl oz dry white wine
75 ml/3 fl oz double cream
500 g/1 lb spaghetti
large handful of flat leaf parsley, chopped
salt and pepper
freshly grated Parmesan cheese, to serve

one To wash the vongole, place them in a colander and submerge in a bowl of cold water. Shake vigorously, then lift out the colander and replace with fresh water. Repeat until the vongole are clean, then drain well. Check the vongole and discard any that are damaged or open.

two Heat the oil in a large saucepan over a low heat, add the garlic and vongole, cover and cook for 3 mins or until all the vongole have opened. Discard any that do not open.

three Lift the vongole out of the pan with a slotted spoon. Remove half of them from their shells and return any liquid to the pan. Set the vongole aside.

four Add the wine and cream to the pan and increase the heat to reduce the sauce.

five Meanwhile, bring a large saucepan of boiling water to the boil. Cook the spaghetti for 3–4 mins if fresh or 8 mins if dried, or according to packet instructions.

six Return the vongole to the sauce, stir well and simmer for 2 mins. Add the parsley and spaghetti, season and mix well, using 2 spoons to combine the spaghetti with the sauce. Serve with Parmesan.

spaghetti with lobster

preparation time **10 mins**
cooking time **10 mins**
total time **20 mins** serves **4**

1 kg/2 lb cooked lobster, cut in half lengthways
4 tablespoons olive oil
2 shallots, chopped
8 plum tomatoes, skinned, deseeded and
   chopped
juice of 1 lemon
300 g/10 oz spaghetti
handful of chives, snipped
salt and pepper

one Remove all the meat from the lobster
and cut it into chunks.
two Heat the oil in a saucepan, add the
shallots and sauté for 3 mins. Add the
tomatoes and lemon juice, season with salt
and pepper and cook for a further 3 mins.
three Meanwhile, bring a large saucepan
of water to the boil. Cook the spaghetti for
3–4 mins if fresh or 8 mins if dried, or
according to packet instructions.
four Add the lobster to the tomato sauce
and stir, then reduce the heat and cook for
4 mins.
five Drain the pasta well. Add the sauce
to the pasta with the chives, toss with
2 wooden spoons and serve immediately.

This dish makes an excellent
quick supper to serve to friends –
the addition of lobster makes it
really special.

tagliatelle with crab sauce

preparation time **5 mins**
cooking time **15 mins**
total time **20 mins** serves **4**

2 tablespoons olive oil
2 shallots, chopped
200 g/7 oz crab meat
1–2 pinches of crushed dried chillies
grated rind and juice of 1 lemon
300 g/10 oz tagliatelle
4 tablespoons double cream
handful of chives, snipped
salt and pepper
75 g/3 oz Parmesan cheese, freshly grated,
   to serve

one Heat the oil in a saucepan, add the
shallots and sauté gently until soft, but do
not brown.
two Add the crab meat, chillies, lemon rind
and juice and salt and pepper to taste.
three Bring a large saucepan of water to the
boil and cook the tagliatelle for 3–4 mins if
fresh or 6 mins if dried, or according to
packet instructions.
four Add the cream to the crab mixture and
bring to the boil.
five Drain the tagliatelle well. Add the chives
to the crab mixture.
six Add the sauce to the tagliatelle, mix well
and serve with a bowl of grated Parmesan.

pappardelle with prosciutto and porcini

preparation time **10 mins**
cooking time **15 mins**
total time **25 mins** serves **4**

2 tablespoons olive oil
1 garlic clove, crushed
250 g/8 oz porcini, sliced
250 g/8 oz prosciutto
300 g/10 oz pappardelle
150 ml/¼ pint whipping cream
handful of flat leaf parsley, chopped
75 g/3 oz Parmesan cheese, freshly grated
salt and pepper

one Heat the oil in a saucepan, add the garlic and porcini and sauté for 4 mins over a moderate heat.

two Cut the prosciutto into strips; try and keep them separate.

three Meanwhile, bring a large saucepan of water to the boil. Cook the pappardelle for 4 mins if fresh or 9 mins if dried, or according to packet instructions.

four Add the prosciutto, cream and parsley to the porcini and season with salt and pepper. Bring to the boil and simmer for 1 min.

five Drain the pasta, add to the sauce and toss well, using 2 spoons to mix evenly. Sprinkle with the Parmesan, toss well and serve at once.

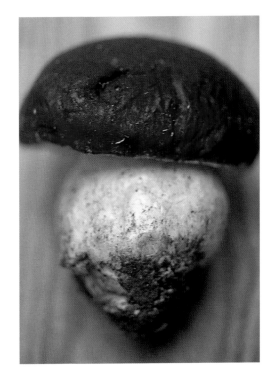

Fresh or dried porcini may be used for this recipe. If you use dried porcini, use 125 g/4 oz and soak them in hot water for 15 mins to rehydrate.

penne with chicken livers

preparation time **10 mins**
cooking time **10 mins**
total time **20 mins** serves **4**

1 yellow pepper, halved, cored and deseeded
300 g/10 oz penne
2 tablespoons olive oil
50 g/2 oz butter
1 red onion, sliced
250 g/8 oz chicken livers, trimmed
1 rosemary sprig, chopped
salt and pepper
75 g/3 oz Parmesan cheese, freshly grated,
    to serve

one Place the yellow pepper under a preheated hot grill for 5 mins, or until the skin is blistered and black. Allow to cool, then peel away the skin. Cut the flesh into long strips.

two Meanwhile, bring a large saucepan of water to the boil. Cook the penne for 4 mins if fresh or 8 mins if dried, or according to packet instructions.

three Heat the oil and butter in a large frying pan, add the onion and chicken livers and cook over a high heat until browned all over. Add the rosemary and season with salt and pepper. Do not overcook the chicken livers as this dries them out and makes them hard; they are best still pink in the middle.

four Drain the penne, add the chicken liver sauce and toss well. Serve immediately with a bowl of freshly grated Parmesan.

spaghetti carbonara

preparation time **10 mins**
cooking time **15 mins**
total time **25 mins** serves **4**

1 tablespoon olive oil
175 g/6 oz smoked bacon, rinded and
    cut into strips
1 garlic clove, crushed
300 g/10 oz spaghetti
4 tablespoons double cream
3 egg yolks
75 g/3 oz Parmesan cheese, freshly grated
salt and pepper

one Heat the oil in a saucepan, add the bacon and cook gently for 3 mins. Add the garlic and cook for 1 min.

two Bring a large saucepan of water to the boil and cook the spaghetti for 3–4 mins if fresh or 8 mins if dried, or according to packet instructions. Drain and return the pasta to the pan.

three Beat the cream and egg yolks together in a bowl, add to the bacon and mix well over a low heat.

four Add the sauce and Parmesan to the pasta, season with salt and pepper and toss well with 2 spoons. Serve immediately.

orecchiette with spicy tomato and pancetta sauce

preparation time **5 mins**
cooking time **20 mins**
total time **25 mins** serves **4**

2 tablespoons olive oil
1 onion, chopped
2 garlic cloves, crushed and chopped
125 g/4 oz pancetta, chopped
400 g/13 oz can chopped tomatoes
½–1 teaspoon crushed dried chillies
125 ml/4 fl oz red wine
300 g/10 oz orecchiette
handful of flat leaf parsley, chopped
handful of basil, chopped
salt and pepper
75 g/3 oz Parmesan cheese shavings,
    to garnish

one Heat the oil in a saucepan, add the onion, garlic and pancetta and sauté for 5 mins.
two Add the tomatoes, chillies and wine and simmer for 15 mins or until the sauce is rich and thick.
three Bring a large saucepan of water to the boil and cook the orecchiette for 3 mins if fresh or 6 mins if dried, or according to packet instructions. Drain well.
four Stir the parsley, basil and salt and pepper to taste into the sauce. Add to the pasta and toss well. Garnish with some of the Parmesan shavings and serve the remainder in a separate bowl at the table.

pasta bake with spinach and ham

preparation time **15 mins**
cooking time **15 mins**
total time **30 mins** serves **4**

2 tablespoons olive oil, plus extra
    for oiling
1 onion, chopped
1 garlic clove, crushed and chopped
750 g/1½ lb fresh spinach, washed and
    chopped
pinch of grated nutmeg
8 sheets of fresh lasagne
250 g/8 oz ham, chopped into large chunks
125 g/4 oz packet buffalo mozzarella cheese,
    thinly sliced
125 g/4 oz fontina cheese, grated
salt and pepper

one Heat the oil in a saucepan, add the onion and garlic and sauté for 3 mins.
two Add the spinach and mix well. Cook for 2 mins over a moderate heat, just so that the spinach starts to wilt. Add nutmeg to taste and season with salt and pepper.
three Lightly oil a large, shallow baking dish, place a layer of lasagne at the bottom, followed by a layer of the spinach mixture, a layer of ham, then a layer of mozzarella. Repeat until all the ingredients are used up, finishing with a layer of lasagne and the grated fontina cheese.
four Place at the top of a preheated oven, 200°C (400°F), Gas Mark 6, and bake for 15 mins until golden brown and bubbling.

Because this dish uses fresh lasagne and is loosely
layered, it cooks through much more quickly than
traditional baked lasagne.

risotto

Traditionally, risotto is served in small portions in large, wide-rimmed soup plates and topped with grated Parmesan or pecorino cheese. Sometimes risottos are simple with just the addition of fresh herbs; other times they are more substantial, cooked with seafood, meat or vegetables. It is essential that the short-grained arborio or carnaroli rices are used for risottos.

risotto alla milanese

preparation time **5 mins**
cooking time **20 mins**
total time **25 mins** serves **4**

1 litre/1¾ pints chicken stock
75 g/3 oz butter
1 tablespoon olive oil
2 onions, finely diced
425 g/14 oz arborio or carnaroli rice
½ teaspoon saffron threads
125 ml/4 fl oz dry vermouth or
    white wine
125 g/4 oz Parmesan cheese, freshly grated
salt and pepper

one Place the stock in a saucepan and
simmer gently.
two Melt 50 g/2 oz of the butter with the oil
in a large, heavy-based saucepan, add the
onions and sauté for 5 mins.
three Add the rice and stir well to coat each
grain with the butter and oil. Add enough
stock to just cover the rice and stir well.
Simmer gently, stirring frequently.
four When most of the liquid is absorbed,
add more stock and the saffron and stir well.
Continue adding the stock in stages and
stirring until it is absorbed.
five Finally, add the vermouth or wine,
Parmesan and the remaining butter in small
knobs and season with salt and pepper.
Stir well and serve immediately.

green risotto

preparation time **10 mins**
cooking time **20 mins**
total time **30 mins** serves **4**

1 litre/1¾ pints vegetable stock
125 g/4 oz butter
1 tablespoon olive oil
1 garlic clove, crushed and chopped
1 onion, finely diced
300 g/10 oz arborio or carnaroli rice
125 g/4 oz green beans, trimmed and cut into
    short lengths
125 g/4 oz shelled peas
125 g/4 oz shelled broad beans
125 g/4 oz asparagus, trimmed and cut into
    short lengths
125 g/4 oz baby spinach, chopped
75 ml/3 fl oz dry vermouth or white wine
2 tablespoons chopped parsley
125 g/4 oz Parmesan cheese, freshly grated
salt and pepper

one Place the stock in a saucepan and
simmer gently.
two Melt half of the butter with the oil in
a heavy-based saucepan, add the garlic and
onion and sauté gently for 5 mins.
three Add the rice and stir well to coat
each grain with the butter and oil. Add
enough stock to just cover the rice and stir
well. Simmer gently, stirring frequently.
four When most of the liquid is absorbed,
add more stock and stir well. Continue
adding the stock in stages and stirring
until it is absorbed. Add the vegetables
and vermouth or wine with the final amount
of stock, mix well and cook for 2 mins.
five Remove the pan from the heat,
season and add the remaining butter,
parsley and Parmesan. Mix well and serve
at once.

Fresh or dried mushrooms may be used for this recipe. If you use dried mushrooms, use 125 g/4 oz and soak them in hot water for 15 mins to rehydrate. Use the excess liquid as stock in the recipe, as it is full of delicious flavours.

risotto with forest mushrooms and sage

preparation time **5 mins**
cooking time **20 mins**
total time **25 mins** serves **4**

1 litre/1¾ pints vegetable stock
125 g/4 oz butter
1 tablespoon olive oil
1 garlic clove, crushed and chopped
1 onion, finely diced
250 g/8 oz forest (wild) mushrooms, e.g.
   morels, porcini, chanterelles or common
   open mushrooms, halved or quartered
300 g/10 oz arborio or carnaroli rice
75 ml/3 fl oz dry white wine
1 tablespoon chopped sage
salt and pepper
125 g/4 oz Parmesan cheese, freshly grated,
   to serve
truffle oil, to drizzle (optional)

one Place the stock in a saucepan and simmer gently.

two Melt half of the butter with the oil in a heavy-based saucepan, add the garlic and onion and sauté gently for 3 mins.

three Add the mushrooms and cook gently for 2 mins. Add the rice and stir well to coat each grain with the butter and oil. Add enough stock to just cover the rice and stir well. Simmer gently, stirring frequently.

four When most of the liquid is absorbed, add more stock. Continue adding the stock in stages and stirring until it is absorbed.

five Add the wine, remaining butter, sage and salt and pepper and stir well. Serve with Parmesan and drizzle with truffle oil, if liked.

red wine risotto

preparation time **5 mins**
cooking time **20 mins**
total time **25 mins** serves **4**

600 ml/1 pint chicken stock
450 ml/¾ pint Valpolicella or other red wine
125 g/4 oz butter
1 tablespoon olive oil
2 garlic cloves, crushed and chopped
2 red onions, chopped
300 g/10 oz arborio or carnaroli rice
250 g/8 oz field mushrooms, sliced
175 g/6 oz Parmesan cheese, freshly grated
salt and pepper

one Place the stock and wine in a large saucepan and simmer gently.

two Melt half of the butter with the oil in a heavy-based saucepan, add the garlic and onions and sauté gently for 5 mins.

three Add the rice and stir well to coat each grain with the butter and oil. Add enough stock to just cover the rice and stir well. Simmer gently, stirring frequently. When most of the liquid is absorbed, add more stock. Continue adding the stock in stages and stirring until it is absorbed.

four When half the stock has been incorporated, add the mushrooms and season with salt and pepper. The rice should be stained with the colour of the wine, giving it a rich, dark red colour.

five When all the stock has been added, and the rice is just cooked with a rich, creamy sauce, add most of the Parmesan and the remaining butter and mix well. Garnish with a little grated Parmesan and serve with the remainder of the bottle of red wine.

green herb risotto

preparation time **5 mins**
cooking time **20 mins**
total time **25 mins** serves **4**

1 litre/1¾ pints chicken or vegetable stock
125 g/4 oz butter
2 tablespoons olive oil
1 garlic clove, crushed and chopped
1 onion, finely chopped
300 g/10 oz arborio or carnaroli rice
handful of parsley, chopped
handful of basil, chopped
handful of oregano, chopped
handful of thyme, chopped
125 g/4 oz Toma cheese, grated
salt and pepper
herb sprigs, to garnish

one Place the stock in a saucepan and simmer gently.

two Melt half of the butter with the oil in a heavy-based saucepan, add the garlic and onion and sauté gently for 3 mins.

three Add the rice and stir well to coat each grain with the butter and oil. Add enough stock to just cover the rice and stir well. Simmer gently, stirring frequently. When most of the liquid is absorbed, add more stock. Continue adding the stock in stages and stirring until it is absorbed.

four When all the stock has been added, and the rice is just cooked with a rich, creamy sauce, add the herbs, the remaining butter and the cheese. Season and stir well. Garnish with herb sprigs and serve at once.

Toma cheese is made in the Italian Alps. If you cannot find it, use fontina or Parmesan instead.

butternut squash risotto

preparation time **5 mins**
cooking time **25 mins**
total time **30 mins** serves **4**

1 butternut squash, weighing 1 kg/2 lb
3 tablespoons olive oil
1 litre/1¾ pints hot vegetable stock
125 g/4 oz butter
1 garlic clove, crushed
1 onion, finely diced
300 g/10 oz arborio or carnaroli rice
150 g/5 oz Parmesan cheese, freshly grated
salt and pepper
pumpkin seed oil, to serve

one Top and tail the squash, cut in half around the middle, then pare away the skin from the larger half. Cut in half lengthways, deseed and cut into 5 cm/2 inch dice. Repeat with the other half. Place on a large baking sheet, drizzle with 2 tablespoons of the olive oil and season with salt and pepper. Mix well and cook in the top of a preheated oven, 220°C (425°F), Gas Mark 7, for 15 mins.

two Melt half of the butter with the remaining olive oil in a heavy-based saucepan, add the garlic and onion and sauté gently for 5 mins.

three Add the rice and stir well to coat each grain with the butter and oil. Add enough of the hot stock to just cover the rice and stir well. Simmer gently, stirring frequently. When most of the liquid is absorbed, add more hot stock. Continue adding the stock in stages and stirring until it is absorbed.

four Add the squash with the Parmesan, remaining butter and salt and pepper and stir gently. Serve drizzled with pumpkin seed oil.

seafood risotto

preparation time **10 mins**
cooking time **20 mins**
total time **30 mins** serves **4**

1 litre/1¾ pints fish stock
good pinch of saffron threads
125 g/4 oz butter
1 tablespoon olive oil
3 shallots, chopped
1 garlic clove, crushed and chopped
300 g/10 oz arborio or carnaroli rice
125 g/4 oz scallops, shelled and prepared
125 g/4 oz squid, cleaned and cut into rings
125 g/4 oz peeled prawns
2 tablespoons chopped flat leaf parsley
75 ml/3 fl oz white wine or dry vermouth
125 g/4 oz Parmesan cheese, freshly grated
salt and pepper

one Place the stock and saffron in a
saucepan and simmer gently.
two Melt half of the butter with the oil in
a heavy-based saucepan, add the shallots
and garlic and sauté gently for 5 mins.
three Add the rice and stir well to coat each
grain with the butter and oil. Add enough
stock to just cover the rice and stir well.
Simmer gently, stirring frequently. When
almost all the liquid is absorbed, add more
stock. Continue adding the stock in stages
and stirring until it is absorbed.
four When half the stock has been
incorporated, add the seafood. Increase the
heat a little and add the remaining stock by
the ladle, stirring carefully.
five When all the stock is absorbed, add the
parsley, remaining butter, wine or vermouth,
half of the Parmesan and salt and pepper.
Serve with the remaining Parmesan.

spinach and lemon risotto

preparation time **5 mins**
cooking time **20 mins**
total time **25 mins** serves **4**

1 litre/1¾ pints vegetable stock
125 g/4 oz butter
1 tablespoon olive oil
2 shallots, finely chopped
300 g/10 oz arborio or carnaroli rice
500 g/1 lb spinach, chopped
grated rind and juice of 1 lemon
125 g/4 oz Parmesan cheese, freshly grated
salt and pepper
grated lemon rind, to garnish (optional)

one Place the stock in a saucepan and
simmer gently.
two Melt half of the butter with the oil in a
heavy-based saucepan, add the shallots and
sauté gently for 3 mins.
three Add the rice and stir well to coat each
grain with the butter and oil. Add enough
stock to just cover the rice and stir well.
Simmer gently, stirring frequently. When
almost all the liquid is absorbed, add more
stock. Continue adding the stock in stages
and stirring until it is absorbed.
four Before you add the last of the stock,
stir in the spinach, lemon rind and juice and
salt and pepper to taste. Increase the heat,
stir well and add the remaining stock and
butter. Allow to cook for a few mins, then
add half of the Parmesan and mix in well.
Serve garnished with the remaining
Parmesan and grated lemon rind, if liked.

The secret of a good risotto is to cook it
very slowly over a low heat until all the
liquid has been absorbed and the rice is
plump and tender.

pizza and polenta

Naples is reputed to be the original home of the pizza, but pizzas are now found all over Italy. Polenta is a yellow maize flour from northern Italy which can be baked, grilled, used as an accompaniment or is delicious with the addition of cheese.

It is very important to cook the pizza bases in a very hot oven, so do make sure to turn the oven on well in advance.

quick pizza base

preparation time **10 mins**
cooking time **see recipes** makes **4**

250 g/8 oz self-raising flour
1 teaspoon salt
150 ml/¼ pint warm water

one Place the flour and salt in a large bowl and mix well. Slowly add the water and mix to form a soft dough. When it has bound together, mix the dough with your hands into a ball. Turn the dough out on a lightly floured surface and knead until it is smooth and soft.

two Divide the dough into 4 and, with your hands and a rolling pin, flatten it as thinly as possible. The pizza rounds do not have to be exact circles as that is one of the charms of making your own pizzas! Make the pizzas just a bit smaller than your serving plates and as thin as you can.

classic tomato pizza

preparation time **8–10 mins**,
plus preparing the pizza base
cooking time **10 mins**
total time **30 mins** serves **4**

1 recipe Quick Pizza Base (see left)
3 tablespoons olive oil
2 red onions, sliced finely
2 garlic cloves, crushed
2 x 400 g/13 oz cans chopped tomatoes
1 teaspoon red wine vinegar
sugar, to taste
8 anchovy fillets, cut into thin lengths
2 tablespoons pitted black olives
1 tablespoon capers
250 g/8 oz mozzarella cheese, sliced
salt and pepper

one Roll out the dough to 4 circles or a large square.

two Heat the oil in a large saucepan, add the onions and garlic and sauté for 3 mins. Add the tomatoes, vinegar and sugar and season with salt and pepper. Increase the heat and simmer the mixture until it has reduced by half to make a thick and rich tomato sauce.

three Place the pizza bases on warmed baking sheets, spoon over the sauce and spread to the edge of the bases with the back of the spoon.

four Arrange the anchovies on the pizzas, sprinkle with the olives and capers and finally add the mozzarella. Put the pizzas into a preheated oven, 230°C (450°F), Gas Mark 8, and cook for 10 mins until golden and sizzling.

artichoke and goats' cheese pizza

preparation time **8–10 mins**,
plus preparing the pizza base
cooking time **10–15 mins**
total time **30 mins** serves **4**

1 recipe Quick Pizza Base (see page 50)
2 onions, finely sliced
1 kg/2 lb artichokes in oil
2 tablespoons pitted black olives
175 g/6 oz mild goats' cheese, cut into thin
    slices or crumbled
handful of oregano, chopped
salt and pepper

one Put the pizza bases on to warmed
baking sheets.
two Mix together the onions and artichokes
and season well with salt and pepper.
three Divide the mixture between the bases
and spread over evenly. Sprinkle with the
olives and top with the goats' cheese,
oregano and salt and pepper. Put the pizzas
into a preheated oven, 230°C (450°F), Gas
Mark 8, and bake for 10–15 mins.

fresh wild mushroom pizza

preparation time **8–10 mins**,
plus preparing the pizza base
cooking time **10–15 mins**
total time **30 mins** serves **4**

1 recipe Quick Pizza Base (see page 50)
olive oil, for brushing
2 onions, finely sliced
2 garlic cloves, crushed
250 g/8 oz wild mushrooms, sliced
drizzle of truffle oil
salt and pepper
handful of flat leaf parsley, chopped,
    to garnish

one Put the pizza bases on to warmed
baking sheets and brush them lightly with
olive oil.
two Mix together the onions, garlic and
mushrooms and season with salt and
pepper. Spread the mixture over the pizzas
and drizzle with a scant amount of truffle
oil. Put the pizzas into a preheated oven,
230°C (450°F), Gas Mark 8, and bake for
10–15 mins.
three Sprinkle the pizzas with parsley and
serve at once.

The addition of 50 g/2 oz of wild mushrooms, such as chanterelles, to this pizza makes it really special.

fresh vegetable pizza

preparation time **20 mins**,
plus preparing the pizza base
cooking time **10 mins**
total time **30 mins** serves **4**

1 recipe Quick Pizza Base (see page 50)
5 tablespoons olive oil
2 garlic cloves, crushed
1 red onion, finely sliced
2 courgettes, thinly sliced lengthways
1 red pepper, cored, deseeded and cut into
  thin strips
1 yellow pepper, cored, deseeded and cut into
  thin strips
4 plum tomatoes, skinned, cored and cut into
  small wedges
500 g/1 lb asparagus, trimmed
4 thyme sprigs, separated into leaves
handful of basil leaves, roughly torn
salt and pepper
75 g/3 oz fresh Parmesan shavings (optional),
  to serve

one Put the pizza bases on to warmed
baking sheets, brush with a little oil, then
arrange the vegetables on the bases,
sprinkling them with the thyme leaves and
roughly torn basil.
two Season the pizzas generously with salt
and pepper, drizzle with the remaining oil
and bake at the top of a preheated oven,
230°C (450°F), Gas Mark 8, for 10 mins. The
vegetables should be slightly charred around
the edges as this adds to the flavour. Serve
with fresh Parmesan shavings, if liked.

anchovy and red pepper pizza

preparation time **8 mins**,
plus preparing the pizza base
cooking time **10 mins**
total time **18 mins** serves **4**

4 tablespoons olive oil
2 red onions, sliced
4 red peppers, cored, deseeded and cut into
  strips
2 garlic cloves, crushed
1 recipe Quick Pizza Base (see page 50)
50 g/2 oz can anchovies, drained
handful of marjoram, chopped
1 tablespoon black olives, pitted and chopped
250 g/8 oz buffalo mozzarella, sliced
salt and pepper

one Heat the oil in a saucepan, add the
onions and red peppers and cook for 5 mins
or until soft. Add the garlic and mix well.
two Put the pizza bases on to warmed
baking sheets, then spoon and spread the
cooked peppers over them. Arrange the
anchovies on top, sprinkle with salt and
pepper to taste, chopped marjoram and
olives and add the slices of mozzarella.
three Put the pizzas into a preheated oven,
230°C (450°F), Gas Mark 8, and bake for
about 10 mins.

spinach, parma ham and egg pizza

preparation time **15 mins**,
plus preparing the pizza base
cooking time **13–15 mins**
total time **30 mins** serves **4**

1 recipe Quick Pizza Base (see page 50)
olive oil, for brushing and drizzling
2 onions, finely sliced
2 garlic cloves, peeled and sliced
4 tomatoes, skinned and sliced
250 g/8 oz spinach, cooked and chopped
8 slices of Parma ham, cut into strips
1 tablespoon black olives, pitted and chopped
4 eggs
salt and pepper

one Put the pizza bases on to warmed
baking sheets. Brush them lightly with oil
and season with salt and pepper.
two Mix together the onions, garlic,
tomatoes, spinach, Parma ham and olives
and spread over the bases, making a nest in
the middle of each one for the egg.
three Drizzle the pizzas with the oil and
season with salt and pepper. Put into a
preheated oven, 230°C (450°F), Gas Mark 8,
and cook for 10 mins, then remove
from the oven and crack the eggs into the
nests. Return the pizzas to the oven for 3–5
mins, then serve immediately. If you like
your egg hard, put it on to the vegetable
topping when it first goes in the oven.

creamed polenta with dolcelatte and mascarpone

preparation time **5 mins**
cooking time **about 15 mins**
total time **20 mins** serves **4**

600 ml/1 pint water
150 g/5 oz quick cooking polenta flour
50 g/2 oz butter
2 tablespoons olive oil
175 g/6 oz dolcelatte and mascarpone torta
handful of oregano, chopped
salt and pepper

one Heat the water in a saucepan to a
gentle simmer, add the polenta and beat
well for 1–2 mins until it is a smooth paste.
two Turn the heat down and continue to
cook the polenta until it thickens, stirring
constantly so that it does not catch on the
bottom of the pan or form a skin on the top;
it needs to cook in this way for 6–8 mins.
three When it is thick and cooked, add salt
and pepper to taste, butter and oil and mix
well. The dolcelatte and mascarpone torta is
very creamy and wet; break it up into small
pieces and add to the polenta with the
oregano. Mix well.
four The polenta should now be the
consistency of soft mashed potatoes. Serve
on its own or with grilled chicken breasts.

Polenta has to be stirred continuously during cooking or it will become lumpy.
Use instant or quick cooking polenta for these recipes.

baked polenta with fontina

preparation time **10 mins**
cooking time **20 mins**
total time **30 mins** serves **4**

600 ml/1 pint water
150 g/5 oz quick cooking polenta flour
125 g/4 oz butter, plus extra for greasing
handful of marjoram, chopped
200 g/7 oz fontina cheese, grated
salt and pepper

SAUCE
3 tablespoons olive oil
2 garlic cloves, crushed
1 onion, chopped
400 g/13 oz can chopped tomatoes
1 thyme sprig
1 teaspoon vinegar
1 teaspoon sugar

one Heat the water in a saucepan to a gentle simmer, add the polenta and beat well for 1–2 mins until it is a smooth paste.
two Turn the heat down and continue to cook the polenta until it thickens, stirring constantly so that it does not catch on the bottom of the pan or form a skin on the top; it needs to cook in this way for 6–8 mins.
three When the polenta is thick and cooked, add the butter, chopped marjoram and salt and pepper to taste. Mix well. Place the polenta on a chopping board, roll out to 1.5 cm/¾ inch thick and allow to set for 5 mins. Alternatively, shape into a loaf shape and slice into 1.5 cm/¾ inch thick slices.
four To make the sauce, heat the oil in a saucepan, add the garlic and onion and sauté for 3 mins.
five Add the tomatoes, thyme, vinegar and sugar. Season with salt and pepper and simmer for 10 mins over a moderate to high heat until the tomatoes reduce to make a thick sauce.
six Butter a shallow ovenproof dish, cut the polenta into squares and line the bottom of the dish with half of the squares. Sprinkle over half of the grated fontina. Spoon over half of the sauce and top with the remaining polenta. Add the remaining sauce and the remaining grated fontina and bake in a preheated oven, 200°C (400°F), Gas Mark 6, for 10–15 mins until the cheese is golden and the sauce is bubbling.

grilled polenta with mushrooms and parma ham

preparation time **5 mins**
cooking time **25 mins**
total time **30 mins** serves **4**

600 ml/1 pint water
150 g/5 oz quick cooking polenta flour
125 g/4 oz butter
1 tablespoon olive oil
1 garlic clove, crushed
375 g/12 oz mushrooms, sliced
½ teaspoon chopped thyme
125 ml/4 fl oz dry white wine
8 thin slices of Parma ham
salt and pepper

one Heat the water in a saucepan to a gentle simmer, add the polenta and beat well for 1–2 mins until it is a smooth paste.

two Turn the heat down and continue to cook the polenta until it thickens, stirring constantly so that it does not catch on the bottom of the pan or form a skin on the top; it needs to cook in this way for 6–8 mins.

three When the polenta is thick and cooked, add half of the butter and season with salt and pepper. Mix well. Place the polenta on a chopping board, roll out to 1.5 cm/¾ inch thick and allow to set for 5 mins.

four Melt the remaining butter in a saucepan with the oil. Add the garlic, mushrooms and thyme. Sauté for 10 mins with the wine, to keep them moist. Season.

five Cut the polenta into wedges. Cook on a preheated griddle pan for 5 mins each side.

six Serve with the Parma ham draped over and mushrooms spooned over to one side.

rich polenta salad

preparation time **10 mins**
cooking time **20 mins**
total time **30 mins** serves **4**

600 ml/1 pint water
150 g/5 oz quick cooking polenta flour
25 g/1 oz butter
250 g/8 oz goats' cheese, rind removed
1 small radicchio lettuce, separated into leaves
125 g/4 oz rocket
3 tablespoons extra virgin olive oil
1 tablespoon balsamic vinegar
salt and pepper

one Heat the water in a saucepan to a gentle simmer, add the polenta and beat well for 1–2 mins until it is a smooth paste. Turn the heat down and continue to cook the polenta until it thickens, stirring constantly so that it does not catch on the bottom of the pan or form a skin on the top; it needs to cook in this way for 6–8 mins.

two When the polenta is thick and cooked, add the butter and season with salt and pepper. Mix well. Place the polenta on a chopping board, roll out to 1.5 cm/¾ inch thick and allow to set for 5 mins.

three Thinly slice or crumble the goats' cheese and arrange it on the polenta, then cut the polenta into bars or wedges. Place the polenta under a preheated grill and cook until the cheese has melted and starts to bubble.

four Put the radicchio leaves and the rocket into a bowl. Add the oil and vinegar and season with salt and pepper, then toss the leaves until coated. Arrange the salad leaves on individual plates and place the polenta bars on top.

The best goats' cheese to use for this
recipe is the rindless variety. Hard crusted
goats' cheese can be used, but it is not
as easy to spread.

salads

The majority of salads in this chapter can be main meals in their own right, but many make great accompaniments or starters, too.

When making this delicious but very simple salad dish, do try and cut all the ingredients into a similar size. This salad makes a great starter or a side dish to serve with a summer fish supper.

panzanella

preparation time **15 mins**
total time **15 mins** serves **4**

4 slices of ciabatta bread
4 ripe tomatoes
½ cucumber, peeled
1 red onion
handful of chopped flat leaf parsley
1 tablespoon chopped black olives
4 tablespoons extra virgin olive oil
1–2 tablespoons wine vinegar
juice of ½ lemon
salt and pepper

one Cut or tear the bread into small pieces and place them in a large bowl.
two Remove the green core from the tomatoes. Cut them up and add to the pieces of bread.
three Cut the cucumber into quarters lengthways and then into cubes. Add to the salad. Chop the onion and add to the bowl with the parsley and olives.
four Mix together the oil, vinegar and lemon juice and season with salt and pepper. Pour the dressing over the salad and mix well. Cover and leave to stand at room temperature for at least 1 hour before serving, to allow all the flavours to mingle.

caesar salad

preparation time **20 mins**
cooking time **5 mins**
total time **25 mins** serves **4**

1 garlic clove, crushed
4 anchovy fillets, chopped
juice of 1 lemon
2 teaspoons dry English mustard
1 egg yolk
200 ml/7 fl oz extra virgin olive oil
vegetable oil, for frying
3 slices of country bread, cubed
1 Cos lettuce, washed and torn into pieces
3 tablespoons freshly grated Parmesan cheese
pepper

one Place the garlic, anchovy fillets, lemon juice, mustard and egg yolk in a small mixing bowl and season with pepper. With a hand-held blender or small whisk, mix well until combined. Slowly drizzle in the olive oil, mixing all the time to form a thick, creamy sauce. If the sauce becomes too thick, add a little water.
two Heat the vegetable oil in a frying pan. Test with a small piece of bread to see if it is hot enough; if the bread sizzles, add the croûtons, turning them when they are golden. When they are cooked, transfer them to a plate lined with kitchen paper to absorb the excess oil.
three Put the lettuce into a large bowl, pour over the dressing and 2 tablespoons of the Parmesan and mix well.
four Serve the salad in a large bowl or on individual plates, sprinkled with the croûtons and the remaining Parmesan.

All the ingredients for this dish can be prepared in
advance, but never mix the salad until it is needed,
as the lettuce will go soggy.

This salad makes a tasty supper in its
own right as well as being an ideal
accompaniment to grilled meat or fish.

white bean and sun-dried tomato salad

preparation time **10 mins**
cooking time **5 mins**
total time **15 mins** serves **4**

2 tablespoons olive oil
1 onion, sliced
1 garlic clove, crushed and chopped
425 g/14 oz can white beans, drained
125 g/4 oz sun-dried tomatoes in oil, drained
  and roughly chopped
1 tablespoon chopped black olives
2 teaspoons chopped capers
2 teaspoons chopped thyme
1 tablespoon extra virgin olive oil
juice of ½ lemon
salt and pepper

one Heat the olive oil in a frying pan, add
the onion and garlic and sauté over a high
heat, stirring, to gain a little colour. When
they are golden, remove from the pan.
two Put the beans into a mixing bowl
and stir in the onion and garlic. Add the
sun-dried tomatoes, olives, capers, thyme,
extra virgin olive oil, lemon juice and salt
and pepper to taste and mix well. Check
the seasoning and serve.

tomato and green bean salad

preparation time **10 mins**
cooking time **2 mins**
total time **12 mins** serves **4**

250 g/8 oz mixed red and yellow baby
  tomatoes, plum if possible
250 g/8 oz thin green beans, topped and tailed
handful of mint, chopped
1 garlic clove, crushed and chopped
4 tablespoons extra virgin olive oil
1 tablespoon balsamic vinegar
salt and pepper

one Cut the baby tomatoes in half and place
in a large bowl.
two Cook the green beans in boiling water
for 2 mins, then drain well and place in the
large bowl with the tomatoes.
three Add the chopped mint, garlic, oil and
balsamic vinegar. Season with salt and
pepper and mix well. Serve warm or cold.

caponata

preparation time **10 mins**
cooking time **20 mins**
total time **30 mins** serves **4**

6 tablespoons olive oil
2 aubergines, cubed
1 red onion, chopped
3 celery sticks, chopped
5 tomatoes, skinned and roughly chopped
3 tablespoons red wine vinegar
1 tablespoon sugar
1 tablespoon capers
50 g/2 oz black olives, pitted
handful of flat leaf parsley, chopped
salt and pepper

one Heat the oil in a saucepan, add the aubergines and fry until golden and soft. Remove from the pan and drain on kitchen paper.
two Add the onion and celery to the pan and sauté for 6 mins until soft but not brown.
three Add the tomatoes and cook for 3 mins, then add the vinegar, sugar, capers, olives, parsley and salt and pepper to taste. Simmer for 5 mins. Remove the pan from the heat, add the aubergines and mix well. Allow to cool, then serve.

aubergine, tomato and mozzarella mountains

preparation time **10 mins**
cooking time **10 mins**
total time **20 mins** serves **4**

1 aubergine, cut into 8 slices
4 beef tomatoes, skinned, then cut into
   8 slices
250 g/8 oz packet buffalo mozzarella,
   cut into 8 slices
2 tablespoons olive oil, plus extra for oiling
salt and pepper
mint sprigs, to garnish
Pesto (see page 16), to serve

one Arrange the aubergine slices on a preheated hot griddle pan or under a hot grill and cook until browned on both sides.
two Lightly oil a baking sheet.
three To prepare the stacks, place 4 of the aubergine slices on the baking sheet. Put a tomato slice and a mozzarella slice on each one, then make a second layer of aubergine, tomato and mozzarella, sprinkling each layer with salt and pepper as you go. Skewer with a cocktail stick through the centre to hold the stacks together.
four Place the stacks in a preheated oven, 190°C (375°F), Gas Mark 5, and cook for 10 mins.
five To serve, transfer the stacks on to individual serving plates and carefully remove the cocktail sticks. Drizzle with a little oil and top with a spoonful of Pesto (see page 16). Garnish with mint sprigs and serve warm or at room temperature.

Serve these 'mountains' with crusty Italian bread
to mop up the delicious pesto juices.

Serve this aubergine salad as a starter
or as an accompaniment.

piedmont peppers

preparation time **5 mins**, plus cooling
cooking time **25 mins**
total time **30 mins** serves **4**

4 red peppers
4–8 anchovy fillets
4 tomatoes, skinned and quartered
4 tablespoons olive oil, plus extra for oiling
salt and pepper

TO GARNISH
handful of green or red basil, roughly torn
125 g/4 oz Parmesan cheese

one Cut the red peppers in half lengthways.
Cut through the stalk first and then the
flesh. I always leave the stalk on as it looks
attractive. Remove the seeds and white ribs.
two Lightly oil a baking sheet and place the
peppers on it, skin side down.
three Cut the anchovies into halves or
quarters lengthways, depending how much
you like anchovies.
four Put 2 tomato quarters into each red
pepper, make an anchovy cross on top and
drizzle with oil. Sprinkle with salt and
pepper, place in a preheated oven, 200°C
(400°F), Gas Mark 6 and cook for 25 mins.
five Allow the peppers to cool, then serve
garnished with torn basil and Parmesan
shavings. Shave the Parmesan straight on
to the peppers, using a mandoline or a
vegetable peeler.

aubergine salad

preparation time **10 mins**, plus cooling
cooking time **15 mins**
total time **25 mins** serves **4**

4 tablespoons olive oil
1 onion, chopped
2 garlic cloves, crushed
2 aubergines, cubed
4 tomatoes, skinned and roughly chopped
4 anchovy fillets, chopped
2 tablespoons pitted black olives
75 g/3 oz pine nuts, toasted
2 tablespoons chopped capers
handful of flat leaf parsley, chopped
salt and pepper

ITALIAN SALAD DRESSING
1 tablespoon white wine vinegar
3 tablespoons olive oil
juice of ½ lemon
1 teaspoon Dijon mustard

one Heat the oil in a saucepan, add the
onion, garlic and aubergines and sauté for
15 mins.
two Meanwhile, make the salad dressing.
Place all the ingredients in a jar with a lid,
season with salt and pepper and shake well.
Set aside.
three Add the tomatoes, anchovies, olives,
pine nuts, capers and parsley to the
aubergine mixture and season with salt and
pepper. Pour in the salad dressing, mix well,
then allow the salad to cool before serving.

rocket, tuna and haricot bean salad

preparation time **15 mins**
total time **15 mins** serves **4**

4 tomatoes, skinned, cored and roughly
   chopped
125 g/4 oz rocket
425 g/14 oz can haricot beans, drained
200 g/7 oz can tuna in olive oil
1 red onion, chopped
125 g/4 oz artichoke hearts in olive oil
2 young celery sticks with leaves, chopped
1 tablespoon pitted black olives
juice of 1 lemon
1 tablespoon red wine vinegar
¼ teaspoon crushed dried chillies
handful of flat leaf parsley, roughly chopped
salt and pepper
warm crusty bread, to serve

one Put the tomatoes into a large salad
bowl with the rocket.
two Stir in the beans and the tuna and its
olive oil, roughly breaking up the tuna into
large flakes. Stir in the chopped onion.
three Add the artichoke hearts and their
olive oil, celery, olives, lemon juice, vinegar,
chillies and parsley and season with salt
and pepper.
four Mix all the ingredients together well
and allow to stand for 30 mins for the
flavours to mingle. Serve at room
temperature with warm crusty bread.

chicken and parmesan salad

preparation time **10 mins**
cooking time **15 mins**
total time **25 mins** serves **4**

2 boneless, skinless chicken breasts
1 garlic clove, crushed
150 ml/¼ pint olive oil
3 anchovy fillets, roughly chopped
juice of ½ lemon
1 teaspoon English mustard powder
1 egg yolk
1 Cos lettuce, torn into pieces
handful of basil, roughly torn
3 slices of ciabatta or white country bread,
   cubed and fried in oil
75 g/3 oz Parmesan cheese
pepper

one Place the chicken breasts on a
preheated hot griddle pan or under a hot
grill and cook on each side for 5 mins.
two Put the garlic, oil, anchovies, lemon
juice, mustard and egg yolk into a food
processor or blender, season with pepper
and process until blended.
three Put the lettuce into a large bowl, pour
in the dressing and toss.
four Arrange the lettuce on serving plates
and sprinkle with torn basil leaves and the
croûtons.
five Slice the chicken into long lengths
and place on top of the lettuce. Shave
the Parmesan on to the chicken with a
mandoline or vegetable peeler and serve.

figs with parma ham

preparation time **5 mins**, plus **5 mins** standing
total time **10 mins** serves **4**

4 figs
juice of ½ lemon
4 tablespoons extra virgin olive oil
handful of basil, roughly torn
12 slices of Parma ham, cut into paper-thin
     slices
salt and pepper

one Cut the figs into quarters and remove
the stems. Place them in a dish with the
lemon juice, oil and roughly torn basil leaves
and season with salt and pepper. Mix well
and allow to stand for 5 mins.
two Arrange the Parma ham on a serving
plate, then spoon the figs over the ham.
Sprinkle with salt and pepper and serve at
room temperature.

This recipe is very simple and relies
heavily on the quality of the
ingredients used, so it is best made
when figs are in season and then
only if they look ripe and delicious.
It is also important to buy your
Parma ham from a delicatessen
where the ham is carved to order.
If you like, the figs can be replaced
with a fragrant, ripe melon, peeled,
deseeded and cut into wedges.

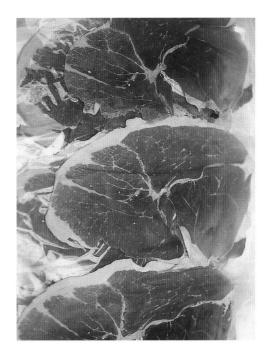

vegetables

In Italy, vegetables appear at many different stages of the meal, as antipasti, in soups, as accompaniments and as main courses. Italy is blessed with an abundance of different vegetables including baby artichokes, asparagus, spinach and fennel.

If you have to wash the spinach, do make sure that it is dry before you start to cook. Place it in a salad spinner or tea towel, and spin it around to disperse any excess water.

quick spinach

preparation time **10 mins**
cooking time **10 mins**
total time **20 mins** serves **4**

1 tablespoon olive oil
1 red onion, sliced
1 garlic clove, crushed
75 g/3 oz pine nuts
4 tomatoes, skinned, cored and roughly
   chopped
1 kg/2 lb spinach, washed and trimmed
50 g/2 oz butter
pinch of nutmeg
salt and pepper

one Heat the oil in a large saucepan, add the onion and garlic and sauté for 5 mins.
two Put the pine nuts into a heavy-based frying pan and dry-fry until browned, stirring constantly as they turn very quickly.
three Add the tomatoes, spinach, butter and nutmeg to the onion and garlic and season with salt and pepper. Turn up the heat to high and mix well. Cook for 3 mins until the spinach has just started to wilt. Remove the pan from the heat, stir in the pine nuts and serve immediately.

fried courgettes with chillies

preparation time **5 mins**
cooking time **10 mins**
total time **15 mins** serves **4**

750 g/1½ lb courgettes, thickly sliced
75 g/3 oz plain flour
olive oil, for frying
50 g/2 oz butter
½ teaspoon crushed dried chillies
2 garlic cloves, crushed
rind and juice of 1 lemon
1 tablespoon green olives, pitted and chopped
salt and pepper

one Dust the courgette slices all over with the flour.
two Heat the oil in a frying pan and fry the courgettes, in batches, for 2 mins on each side until golden. Remove from the pan and keep warm.
three When all the courgettes are cooked, pour off the oil from the pan. Add the butter, chillies, garlic, lemon rind and juice and the olives and heat until the butter is foaming. Pour over the courgettes, season with salt and pepper and toss. Serve immediately.

courgette fritters

preparation time **10 mins**
cooking time **12 mins**
total time **22 mins** serves **4**

500 g/1 lb courgettes, trimmed and grated
1 garlic clove, crushed
50 g/2 oz Parmesan cheese, freshly grated
50 g/2 oz plain flour
1 egg, beaten
olive oil, for frying
salt and pepper
1 lemon, cut into 4 wedges, to serve

one Mix the grated courgettes, garlic, Parmesan, flour and beaten egg together in a large bowl and season with salt and pepper.
two Heat the oil in a frying pan. Place spoonfuls of the courgette mixture in the hot oil and fry for about 4–5 mins on each side or until golden and crispy.
three As the fritters are done, lift them out of the pan with a slotted spoon, pile in a warmed serving dish and keep warm. Keep cooking until all the courgette mixture is used up.
four Serve the fritters sprinkled with salt and accompanied by lemon wedges.

vegetable frittata

preparation time **5 mins**
cooking time **25 mins**
total time **30 mins** serves **4–6**

2 tablespoons olive oil
2 onions, finely sliced
2 garlic cloves, crushed
2 potatoes, boiled and sliced
2 red peppers, cored, deseeded and cut into
  strips
6 courgettes, sliced
1 thyme sprig, chopped
5 eggs, beaten
50 g/2 oz Parmesan cheese, freshly grated
salt and pepper

one Heat the oil in a frying pan with a
heatproof handle. Add the onions, garlic,
potatoes, red peppers and courgettes and
sauté for 5 mins.
two Add the thyme, season with salt and
pepper and mix well. Pour in the beaten eggs
and cook over a moderate heat for 3 mins.
three Sprinkle with the grated Parmesan,
put the pan into a preheated oven, 200°C
(400°F), Gas Mark 6, and cook for 15 mins.
The frittata should be set and golden on top.
four Remove the pan from the oven. Ease
a palette knife all the way around the edge
and under the frittata, slide it on to a large
plate and serve at once.

balsamic braised leeks and peppers

preparation time **5 mins**
cooking time **20 mins**
total time **25 mins** serves **4**

2 tablespoons olive oil
2 leeks, cut into 1 cm/½ inch pieces
1 orange pepper, cored, deseeded and cut into
  1 cm/½ inch chunks
1 red pepper, cored, deseeded and cut
  into 1 cm/½ inch chunks
3 tablespoons balsamic vinegar
handful of flat leaf parsley, chopped
salt and pepper

one Heat the oil in a saucepan, add the
leeks and orange and red peppers and stir
well. Cover the pan and cook very gently for
10 mins.
two Add the balsamic vinegar and cook for a
further 10 mins without a lid. The vegetables
should be brown from the vinegar and all the
liquid should have evaporated.
three Season well, then stir in the parsley
just before serving.

The vegetables in this dish take on a wonderful
brown colour from the balsamic vinegar.

spinach and ricotta frittata

preparation time **5 mins**
cooking time **25 mins**
total time **30 mins** serves **4–6**

3 tablespoons olive oil
2 onions, finely sliced
1 garlic clove, crushed
5 eggs
500 g/1 lb spinach, washed and chopped
175 g/6 oz ricotta cheese
50 g/2 oz pine nuts
25 g/1 oz black olives, pitted and chopped
salt and pepper

one Heat 2 tablespoons of the oil in a frying pan with a heatproof handle, add the onions and garlic and sauté gently for 3 mins; do not brown.
two Beat the eggs in a large bowl and season well with salt and pepper. Add the chopped spinach and crumble in three-quarters of the ricotta. Add the pine nuts and olives and mix well. Add the onions and garlic and mix again.
three Heat the remaining oil in the frying pan, pour in the spinach mixture and cook for 5 mins.
four Sprinkle with the remaining ricotta and season with salt and pepper. Put the pan in a preheated oven, 200°C (400°F), Gas Mark 6, and cook for 15 mins. The frittata should be set and golden on top.
five To serve, ease a palette knife all the way around the edge and under the frittata, then slide it on to a large plate. This dish can be eaten hot or cold.

fennel baked with cream and parmesan

preparation time **5 mins**
cooking time **25 mins**
total time **30 mins** serves **4**

750 g/1½ lb fennel
small knob of butter
250 ml/8 fl oz double cream
75 g/3 oz freshly grated Parmesan cheese
salt and pepper

one Trim the outside leaves from the fennel, remove the hard central core and slice the fennel lengthways. Immerse the leaves in a pan of boiling water and cook for 5 mins. Drain well.
two Butter a shallow ovenproof dish, add the fennel and sprinkle with salt and pepper. Pour over the cream and sprinkle with the Parmesan.
three Place the dish at the top of a preheated oven, 200°C (400°F), Gas Mark 6, and cook for 20 mins. Allow the top of the fennel to go a deep golden brown.

baked young celery with parmesan

preparation time **5 mins**
cooking time **20 mins**
total time **25 mins** serves **4**

25 g/1 oz butter
2 small young heads of celery
handful of oregano, chopped
3 tablespoons olive oil
75 g/3 oz Parmesan cheese, freshly grated
salt and pepper

one Butter a large ovenproof dish. Cut the celery heads into quarters lengthways and place in the prepared dish. Add the oregano, drizzle with oil and season well with salt and pepper.
two Sprinkle the grated Parmesan over the celery and cook in a preheated oven, 200°C (400°F), Gas Mark 6, for 20 mins. The celery should become soft and the cheese golden and crunchy on top.

roast vegetables with olive oil and chillies

preparation time **5 mins**
cooking time **25 mins**
total time **30 mins** serves **4**

4 tablespoons olive oil
250 g/8 oz parsnips, cut into
   equal-sized chunks
250 g/8 oz leeks, cut into 1 cm/½ inch lengths
250 g/8 oz red peppers, cored, deseeded and
   cut into squares
250 g/8 oz aubergines, cut into chunks
½ teaspoon crushed dried chillies
handful of marjoram, chopped
salt and pepper

one Place the oil in a large roasting tin and put it into a preheated oven, 220°C (425°F), Gas Mark 7, for a few mins to warm.
two Add the parsnips to the tin, toss well in the oil, then return the tin to the top of the oven and cook the parsnips for 10 mins.
three Remove the tin from the oven and add the leeks, red peppers, aubergines and crushed chillies. Toss to coat in the olive oil, then return the tin to the oven to cook for a further 15 mins.
four Remove the tin from the oven and add the chopped marjoram and salt and pepper. Mix well and serve immediately.

stuffed aubergines

preparation time **5 mins**
cooking time **25 mins**
total time **30 mins** serves **4**

2 aubergines
4 tablespoons olive oil, plus extra for oiling
8 tomatoes, skinned and chopped
2 garlic cloves, crushed
4 anchovy fillets, chopped
1 tablespoon capers, chopped
handful of basil, chopped
handful of flat leaf parsley, chopped
75 g/3 oz pecorino cheese, grated
2 tablespoons pine nuts, toasted
50 g/2 oz white breadcrumbs
salt and pepper

one Cut the aubergines in half lengthways
and scoop out the flesh without breaking the
skin. Roughly chop the flesh.
two Heat the oil in a frying pan, add the
aubergine shells and sauté them on each
side for 3–4 mins. Place them in a lightly
oiled baking dish. Add the aubergine flesh to
the pan and sauté until golden brown.
three Mix the chopped tomatoes, garlic,
anchovies, capers, basil, parsley, half of the
pecorino cheese, the pine nuts,
breadcrumbs and aubergine flesh together
and season with salt and pepper. Spoon the
mixture into the sautéed aubergine shells,
piling it high. Sprinkle with the remaining
cheese. Place in a preheated oven, 200°C
(400°F), Gas Mark 6, and cook for 20 mins.

baked aubergine and gorgonzola

preparation time **5 mins**
cooking time **25 mins**
total time **30 mins** serves **4**

4 tablespoons olive oil
1 red onion, chopped
2 garlic cloves, crushed
400 g/13 oz can chopped tomatoes
1 red chilli, diced
handful of basil, roughly torn
2 aubergines, thickly sliced
125 g/4 oz Gorgonzola cheese
salt and pepper

one Heat 1 tablespoon of the oil in a
saucepan and sauté the onion and garlic for
3 mins.
two Add the tomatoes and chilli and simmer
for about 8–10 mins until the sauce has
reduced. Add the basil and season well with
salt and pepper.
three Heat the remaining oil in a large frying
pan, add the aubergine slices and fry until
golden on each side.
four Place a layer of aubergines in a shallow
ovenproof dish and spoon over half of the
sauce. Make another layer of aubergines,
then add the rest of the sauce and finally
crumble over the Gorgonzola. Bake in a
preheated oven, 190°C (375°F), Gas Mark 5,
for 15 mins.

sicilian aubergines

preparation time **5 mins**
cooking time **25 mins**
total time **30 mins** serves **4**

4 tablespoons olive oil
2 red onions, sliced
2 garlic cloves, crushed
2 celery sticks, chopped
1 aubergine, cut into small dice
1 yellow pepper, cored, deseeded and
    cut into thin strips
1 red pepper, cored, deseeded and cut
    into thin strips
150 ml/¼ pint passata
2 tablespoons red wine vinegar
6 anchovy fillets, cut into long strips
50 g/2 oz capers, roughly chopped
125 g/4 oz black olives, pitted
75 g/3 oz pine nuts
handful of flat leaf parsley, chopped
pepper

one Heat the oil in a heavy-based saucepan, add the onions, garlic and celery and sauté gently for 3 mins.
two Add the aubergine and yellow and red peppers, turn up the heat and cook for a further 5 mins, stirring constantly.
three Add the passata and vinegar and bring to the boil, then reduce the heat so that the mixture just simmers for 10 mins. Add the anchovies, capers and olives and simmer the mixture for a further 5 mins.
four Meanwhile, put the pine nuts into a heavy-based pan and dry-fry until browned, stirring constantly as they turn very quickly.
five Finally, season the aubergine mixture generously with pepper, add the pine nuts and chopped parsley and mix well. Serve hot or at room temperature.

broccoli with anchovies

preparation time **5 mins**
cooking time **10 mins**
total time **15 mins** serves **4**

75 g/3 oz pine nuts
1 kg/2 lb broccoli, cut into florets
50 g/2 oz butter
juice of 1 lemon
4 anchovy fillets, finely chopped
75 g/3 oz Parmesan cheese, freshly grated
salt and pepper

one Place the pine nuts in a heavy-based frying pan and dry-fry until lightly browned, stirring constantly as they burn very quickly. Set aside.
two Steam the broccoli or plunge it into boiling water for 2 mins, then drain well and transfer to a bowl.
three Melt the butter in a small saucepan, add the lemon juice and anchovies and heat until the butter foams. Pour the melted butter over the broccoli, sprinkle with salt and pepper and toss. To serve, top the broccoli with the Parmesan and pine nuts.

These potatoes are quite delicious and make an excellent accompaniment to fish, or can be served on their own as a starter. Alternatively, use very small potatoes and serve them with drinks.

roast potatoes with rosemary and garlic

preparation time **5 mins**
cooking time **25 mins**
total time **30 mins** serves **4**

750 g/1½ lb medium potatoes, unpeeled
4 tablespoons olive oil
2 tablespoons chopped rosemary
4 garlic cloves, peeled and sliced
salt and pepper

one Cut the potatoes lengthways into quarters and make sure that they are thoroughly dry.
two Put half of the oil into a large roasting tin and place in a preheated oven, 230°C (450°F), Gas Mark 8, to warm through.
three Mix together the remaining oil and the rosemary and toss the potatoes to coat them completely.
four Add the potatoes to the roasting tin in the oven, shake carefully to give an even layer, then place the tin at the top of the oven and roast for 20 mins.
five Remove the tin from the oven and move the potatoes around so that they cook evenly. Scatter the garlic amongst the potatoes, return the tin to the oven and cook for a further 5 mins. Remove the potatoes from the oven, season with salt and pepper and serve immediately.

potatoes wrapped in parma ham

preparation time **5 mins**
cooking time **20 mins**
total time **25 mins** serves **4**

12 small new potatoes, cooked
12 very thin slices of Parma ham
2 tablespoons olive oil
sea salt

one Roll each potato in a slice of Parma ham, patting with your hands to mould the ham to the shape of the potato.
two Lightly oil a roasting tin, add the potatoes and cook in a preheated oven, 200°C (400°F), Gas Mark 6, for 20 mins. Keep an eye on the potatoes while they are cooking as they may need turning or moving around; often the ones on the edge get more colour than the ones in the middle.
three Serve sprinkled with sea salt.

Cavolo nero is an Italian cabbage with extremely long leaves, which is available in most of the larger supermarkets. It is almost the shape of a Cos lettuce, but the leaves are greeny purple in colour. Cavolo nero has a simple cabbage-like flavour but a slightly firmer texture. Like all cabbage, it is best not overcooked.

cavolo nero with pancetta

preparation time **5 mins**
cooking time **10 mins**
total time **15 mins** serves **4**

1 tablespoon olive oil
1 onion, sliced
1 garlic clove, crushed
1 red chilli, cored, deseeded and diced
125 g/4 oz pancetta, diced
1 head of cavolo nero
75 ml/3 fl oz chicken stock
75 g/3 oz Parmesan cheese, coarsely grated
salt and pepper

one Heat the oil in a large saucepan, add the onion, garlic, chilli and pancetta and sauté for 5 mins or until soft.
two To prepare the cavolo nero, trim any wilting leaves, then cut the heads in half lengthways. Remove and discard the hard central stem and roughly chop the leaves.
three Add the cavolo nero to the onion mixture and stir well. Pour in the stock and season with salt and pepper. Cook for 4 mins over a moderate heat, stirring constantly.
four Finally, add the grated Parmesan and serve at once.

braised broad beans and lentils

preparation time **5 mins**
cooking time **25 mins**
total time **30 mins** serves **4**

2 tablespoons olive oil
1 red onion, chopped
2 garlic cloves, crushed
125 g/4 oz pancetta or unsmoked bacon, diced
175 g/6 oz Puy lentils
1 kg/2 lb fresh shelled or frozen broad beans
handful of marjoram, chopped
8 fresh or canned artichoke hearts, prepared or
   drained
50 g/2 oz butter
handful of flat leaf parsley, chopped
salt and pepper

one Heat the oil in a heavy-based saucepan, add the onion, garlic and pancetta or bacon and sauté for 5 mins.
two Add the lentils, beans and marjoram, season with salt and pepper and cover with hot water. Mix well and simmer for 15 mins. The water may need to be topped up during cooking if the mixture is getting too thick and sticking on the bottom of the pan. Keep stirring, just to check that it does not stick.
three Add the artichoke hearts and cook for 5 mins. The mixture should be thick and rich. Finally, stir in the butter and parsley, taste for seasoning and serve immediately.

fish and shellfish

An abundance of fresh fish and shellfish is available in Italy. Chargrilling and simple cooking are the most popular methods of treating fresh fish.

grilled sea bass

preparation time **5 mins**
cooking time **7 mins**
total time **12 mins** serves **4**

extra virgin olive oil
2 x 1 kg/2 lb sea bass, filleted
salt and pepper

TO SERVE
2 lemons, halved
Braised Broad Beans and Lentils (see page 85)

one Lightly oil a baking sheet. Place the
4 sea bass fillets on the baking sheet and
drizzle with oil. Season generously with salt
and pepper and cook under a preheated very
hot grill for 7 mins.
two Serve with lemon halves and Braised
Broad Beans and Lentils (see page 85).

swordfish steaks in white wine and tomatoes

preparation time **10 mins**
cooking time **15 mins**
total time **25 mins** serves **4**

2 tablespoons olive oil
1 red onion, chopped
1 garlic clove, crushed
2 celery sticks, chopped
2 bay leaves
4 tomatoes, skinned and chopped
1 teaspoon sugar
300 ml/½ pint white wine
2 tablespoons chopped oregano
4 x 175g/6 oz swordfish steaks
salt and pepper

one Heat the oil in a pan, add the onion,
garlic and celery and sauté gently for
5 mins.
two Add the bay leaves, tomatoes, sugar,
wine and oregano and season with salt and
pepper. Mix well and bring to a gentle
simmer.
three Add the swordfish steaks and cook for
5 mins, then turn them over and cook on the
other side for a further 5 mins. This dish can
be served straight away, or in hot weather it
is very good at room temperature.

Choose a saucepan that the pieces
of fish will fit into as neatly as possible –
a frying pan may be best.

spicy fried sardines

preparation time **15 mins**
cooking time **10 mins**
total time **25 mins** serves **4**

oil, for deep-frying
125 g/4 oz plain flour
750 g/1½ lb large, fresh sardines, cleaned
4 tablespoons olive oil
5 shallots, sliced
125 ml/4 fl oz white wine vinegar
4 garlic cloves, crushed
large handful of mint leaves, finely chopped
rind and juice of 1 lemon
½ teaspoon crushed dried chillies
salt and pepper

one Heat the oil for deep-frying in a deep saucepan or deep-fat fryer. Season the flour with salt and pepper.

two Dip the sardines into the flour to coat evenly and fry in the hot oil for 2 mins or until golden. Remove and place on a tray lined with kitchen paper to absorb the excess oil. Keep warm.

three Heat 1 tablespoon of the olive oil in a saucepan, add the shallots and sauté for 5 mins, then add the vinegar and cook until nearly half of it has evaporated.

four Transfer the sardines to a warmed serving dish. Add the remaining olive oil, the garlic, mint, lemon rind and juice and chillies to the onion mixture and cook for 1 min. Spoon the sauce over the sardines and sprinkle with salt and pepper. This dish can be served hot or at room temperature.

tuna steaks with sun-dried tomatoes

preparation time **5 mins**
cooking time **15 mins**
total time **20 mins** serves **4**

2 tablespoons olive oil
1 red onion, finely chopped
2 garlic cloves, crushed
1 rosemary sprig, chopped
75 g/3 oz plain flour
4 x 175 g/6 oz tuna steaks
oil, for frying
125 g/4 oz sun-dried tomatoes, chopped
75 ml/3 fl oz red wine
1 tablespoon capers
75 g/3 oz black olives
handful of flat leaf parsley, chopped
salt and pepper
1 lemon, cut into 4 wedges, to serve

one Heat the olive oil in a saucepan, add the onion, garlic and rosemary and sauté gently for 5 mins.

two Season the flour with salt and pepper. Dip the tuna into the flour to coat evenly.

three Heat the oil for frying in a frying pan, add the tuna and cook for 4–5 mins or until golden. Turn over and cook on the other side for a further 4–5 mins. Transfer to a dish lined with kitchen paper and keep warm in the oven.

four Add the sun-dried tomatoes to the sautéed onions and stir well. Turn up the heat to high, add the wine, capers, olives and parsley and season with salt and pepper. Simmer for 2 mins. Serve the sauce with the tuna steaks and lemon wedges.

trout with parmesan and basil dressing

preparation time **10 mins**
cooking time **10 mins**
total time **20 mins** serves **4**

4 tablespoons olive oil
4 x 200 g/7 oz trout fillets
large handful of basil leaves, roughly chopped
1 garlic clove, crushed
125 g/4 oz Parmesan cheese, freshly grated
salt and pepper

one Lightly brush a baking sheet with oil and place under a preheated very hot grill to heat up.
two Put the trout fillets on to the hot tray, sprinkle with salt and pepper and place under the grill for 5 mins.
three Put the basil and garlic into a bowl. Work in the oil using a hand-held blender.
four Remove the fish from the grill and sprinkle with the grated Parmesan. Return to the grill and cook for a further 3–5 mins or until the Parmesan turns golden. Serve with the basil sauce drizzled over the trout fillets.

grilled red mullet with salsa verde

preparation time **10 mins**
cooking time **15 mins**
total time **25 mins** serves **4**

4 x 375 g/12 oz red mullet, scaled and cleaned

SALSA VERDE
125 g/4 oz flat leaf parsley, chopped
125 g/4 oz basil, chopped
5 anchovy fillets, roughly chopped
2 tablespoons capers
2 garlic cloves, crushed
rind and juice of 1 lemon
150 ml/¼ pint olive oil
salt and pepper

one Make 3 slashes across the fish on each side and season with salt and pepper. Place under a preheated very hot grill and cook on each side for 6–8 mins or until cooked.
two To make the salsa verde, put the parsley, basil, anchovies, capers and garlic into a food processor or blender and process to a smooth paste. Add the lemon rind and juice and oil, season with salt and pepper and blend again.
three Remove the fish from the grill and put a spoonful of the salsa verde into each of the slashes on one side of the fish. Serve the remaining salsa verde at the table in a small serving dish.

Salsa verde, literally translated as green sauce, is traditionally
served with 'bollito mista', a north Italian dish of boiled meats
and poultry. It also tastes great on fresh bread.

fish casserole

preparation time **10 mins**
cooking time **15 mins**
total time **25 mins** serves **4**

3 tablespoons olive oil
2 red onions, finely diced
2 garlic cloves, crushed
½ teaspoon crushed dried chillies
200 g/7 oz squid, cleaned and cut into
    thin lengths
200 g/7 oz mussels, scrubbed and debearded
200 g/7 oz clams, cleaned (see page 32)
300 g/10 oz raw tiger prawns in their shells
150 ml/¼ pint fish stock
150 ml/¼ pint dry white wine
½ teaspoon saffron
8 tomatoes, skinned and deseeded
1 bay leaf
1 teaspoon sugar
500 g/1 lb red mullet fillets, cut into
    bite-sized pieces
handful of flat leaf parsley, chopped
salt and pepper

one Heat the oil in a saucepan large enough
to hold all the ingredients. Add the onions
and garlic and sauté gently for 5 mins. Add
the chillies and mix well.
two Add the squid, mussels, clams and
tiger prawns and stir well.
three Add the stock, wine, saffron,
tomatoes, bay leaf and sugar and season
with salt and pepper. Cover the pan and
simmer gently for 5 mins. Discard any
mussels or clams that do not open.
four Add the red mullet, sprinkle with the
parsley and simmer for a further 5 mins,
then serve at once. This is a very simple
dish to make, but finger bowls are
needed as it is very messy to eat. Serve
with Bruschetta (see page 20) and a green
salad.

halibut in paper parcels

preparation time **5 mins**
cooking time **25 mins**
total time **30 mins** serves **4**

1 fennel bulb
4 x 200 g/7 oz halibut fillets
2 shallots, finely chopped
8 pitted black olives
a few sage leaves, torn
4 lemon slices
salt and pepper

one Cut 4 sheets of greaseproof paper large
enough to enclose the fish and vegetables.
two To prepare the fennel, trim the top and
outer leaves, remove the hard central core
and cut the bulb into slices through the root.
Divide evenly between the sheets of
greaseproof paper and put the fish on top.
Sprinkle with the shallots, olives and sage,
season with salt and pepper and finish with
a slice of lemon. The greaseproof paper can
be folded over and rolled at the edges to
seal, but a much easier way is to fold the
paper and staple it. Put the parcels on to a
baking sheet and cook in a preheated oven,
200°C (400°F), Gas Mark 6, for 25 mins.
three Serve these parcels at the table so
that everyone opens their own parcel and
gets a waft of the delicious aroma that
escapes when they are first opened.

roast monkfish with parma ham

preparation time **10 mins**
cooking time **15 mins**
total time **25 mins** serves **4**

4 x 175 g/6 oz monkfish fillets
4 rosemary sprigs
8 slices of Parma ham
2 tablespoons olive oil, plus extra for oiling
1 red onion, chopped
1 garlic clove, crushed
6 tomatoes, skinned, deseeded and roughly
   chopped
1 teaspoon capers, roughly chopped
handful of flat leaf parsley
salt and pepper

one Season the monkfish with salt and
pepper, place the rosemary sprigs on the
fish and wrap the slices of Parma ham
around them. Put the fish in a lightly oiled
baking dish and cook in a preheated oven,
220°C (425°F), Gas Mark 7, for 15 mins.
two Heat half of the oil in a saucepan, add
the onion and garlic and sauté gently for
5 mins.
three Add the tomatoes and capers and mix
well. Then add the remaining oil and parsley
and season with salt and pepper.
four Serve the fish with some of the sauce
spooned over one end.

roast cod with vegetables

preparation time **5 mins**
cooking time **25 mins**
total time **30 mins** serves **4**

750 g/1½ lb cod fillets, skinned
4 potatoes, unpeeled and quartered
6 tomatoes, halved
1 red onion, quartered
1 fennel bulb, cut into wedges
2 garlic cloves, crushed
75 g/3 oz black olives, pitted
25 g/1 oz green olives, pitted
25 g/1 oz capers
juice of 1 lemon
3 tablespoons olive oil, plus extra for oiling
salt and pepper
handful of flat leaf parsley, chopped,
    to garnish

one Put the cod, potatoes, tomatoes, onion and fennel into a large, lightly oiled dish. Try and arrange them in a single layer. Sprinkle with the garlic, olives, capers and lemon juice and season with salt and pepper.
two Drizzle with oil, place in the top of a preheated oven, 230°C (450°F), Gas Mark 8, and roast for 25 mins.
three Garnish with parsley and serve.

mussels with fresh tomato and pepper sauce

preparation time **5 mins**
cooking time **25 mins**
total time **30 mins** serves **4**

1 red pepper
2 tablespoons olive oil
2 red onions, chopped
2 garlic cloves, crushed
6 tomatoes, skinned and chopped
½ teaspoon crushed dried chillies
125 ml/4 fl oz dry white wine
1 kg/2 lb mussels, cleaned and debearded
2 tablespoons capers
large handful of flat leaf parsley, roughly
    chopped
salt and pepper

one To skin the red pepper, first cut off the bottom of the pepper. Put the pepper on a chopping board and slice off 4–5 flat pieces, leaving the seeds and core intact. Place the pepper pieces under a preheated hot grill and leave to blister and blacken, then peel off the skins and roughly chop the flesh.
two Heat the oil in a large, ovenproof casserole, add the onions and garlic and sauté gently for 5 mins; do not brown.
three Add the tomatoes, chillies and wine and simmer for 5 mins to reduce and thicken the sauce.
four Add the mussels and capers and season with salt and pepper. Mix well, cover with a lid and bake in a preheated oven, 200°C (400°F), Gas Mark 6, for 8 mins.
five Discard any mussels that have not opened, then stir in the parsley and serve.

tiger prawns with garlic and herbs

preparation time **5 mins**
cooking time **6 mins**
total time **11 mins** serves **4**

50 g/2 oz butter
2 tablespoons olive oil
750 g/1½ lb peeled raw tiger prawns
1 shallot, finely diced
2 garlic cloves, crushed
75 ml/3 fl oz dry white wine
125 g/4 oz flat leaf parsley, chopped
125 g/4 oz marjoram, chopped
salt and pepper

one Melt the butter with the oil in a frying
pan, add the tiger prawns, shallot and garlic
and sauté for 5 mins or until all the prawns
have turned pink.
two Add the wine, parsley and marjoram
and season with salt and pepper. Mix well
and serve immediately.

This dish goes very well with
egg pasta, or it can be served
on its own with warm ciabatta
bread to mop up all the juices.

pan-fried squid with chillies

preparation time **15 mins**
cooking time **6 mins**
total time **21 mins** serves **4**

1 kg/2 lb small squid, cleaned
4 tablespoons olive oil
3 garlic cloves, crushed
1 red chilli, finely chopped
juice of 1 lemon
handful of flat leaf parsley, chopped
salt and pepper

one Slit the squid down one side and lay
them flat. Score the skin of each one with
a fine criss-cross pattern.
two Mix half of the oil, garlic, chilli and
lemon juice together in a non-metallic bowl
and add the squid. Mix well to coat all over,
cover and marinate for 15 mins.
three Remove the squid from the marinade,
reserving the marinade. Heat a large frying
pan or a wok with the remaining oil until it
is just smoking. Add the squid, season
with salt and pepper and stir well. Cook
over a high heat for 2–3 mins. The squid
will curl up, but just hold them flat for a
few seconds to get a browned outside.
Finally, add the strained marinade and
the parsley to the pan, mix well and serve
at once.

Chop the squid tentacles and use them in this dish as they
look very pretty. Their faint purple colour is subtly
complemented by the red chilli.

poultry, game and meat

High-quality meat and game are available throughout Italy, so often all that is needed is brief cooking and a sprinkling of olive oil, salt and black pepper. Older cuts are simmered in rich wine sauces to produce wonderfully tender dishes.

chicken livers with marsala and oregano

preparation time **5 mins**
cooking time **10 mins**
total time **15 mins** serves **4**

75 g/3 oz butter
50 g/2 oz pancetta or bacon, diced
1 shallot, diced
1 garlic clove, crushed
500 g/1 lb chicken livers, trimmed
175 ml/6 fl oz Marsala
1 tablespoon chopped oregano
salt and pepper
buttered tagliatelle, to serve

one Melt half of the butter in a large frying pan, add the pancetta or bacon, shallot and garlic and sauté gently for 5 mins; do not allow the shallot and garlic to colour. Remove from the pan.

two Melt the remaining butter, add the chicken livers and cook over a high heat for 3 mins until the livers are evenly brown on the outside. Chicken livers are best when cooked until browned on the outside but still pink in the middle.

three Return the shallot mixture to the pan and mix well. Add the Marsala and oregano and season with salt and pepper. Bring quickly to the boil. Serve immediately with buttered tagliatelle.

country chicken

preparation time **10 mins**
cooking time **20 mins**
total time **30 mins** serves **4**

50 g/2 oz butter
2 tablespoons olive oil
4 boneless chicken breasts
1 onion, chopped
½ small head of celery, chopped
1 garlic clove, crushed
½ teaspoon crushed dried chillies
300 ml/½ pint passata
1 bay leaf
thyme sprig
handful of oregano, roughly chopped
salt and pepper

one Melt the butter with the oil in a frying pan. When it is hot, add the chicken breasts and cook on each side for about 5 mins. Let them brown to add flavour to the sauce.

two Remove the chicken with a slotted spoon and set aside. Add the onion, celery, garlic and chillies to the pan and sauté for 5 mins.

three Add the passata, bay leaf and thyme. Season with salt and pepper and stir well. Return the chicken breasts to the sauce and simmer for 10 mins. Just before serving, add the oregano.

roman chicken

preparation time **5 mins**
cooking time **25 mins**
total time **30 mins** serves **4**

4 tablespoons olive oil
2 red onions, sliced
2 garlic cloves, sliced
2 red peppers, cored, deseeded and sliced
2 yellow peppers, cored, deseeded and sliced
½ teaspoon crushed dried chillies
8 boneless chicken thighs
100 ml/3½ fl oz white wine
large handful of basil, roughly torn
salt and pepper

one Heat the oil in a large frying pan, add
the onions, garlic, red and yellow peppers
and chillies and sauté for 5 mins.
two Add the chicken thighs, pushing them
down to the bottom of the pan to seal on
the outside. Cook for a further 5 mins.
three Add the wine and salt and pepper to
taste, cover the pan and cook for about
15 mins over a low heat. Check occasionally
that the chicken and sauce do not stick to
the bottom of the pan and add a little more
wine if necessary.
four Stir in the basil just before serving.

chicken with rosemary and garlic

preparation time **5 mins**, plus marinating
cooking time **15 mins**
total time **25 mins** serves **4**

2 tablespoons olive oil
2 tablespoons white wine vinegar
2 tablespoons chopped rosemary
3 garlic cloves, crushed
1 teaspoon paprika
pared rind of 1 lemon
4 boneless, skinless chicken breasts, cut into
    long thin strips
handful of flat leaf parsley, chopped
salt and pepper

one Mix the oil, vinegar, rosemary, garlic,
paprika and lemon rind together in a bowl
and season with salt and pepper. Add the
chicken and mix well, then leave to
marinate for 10 mins. Alternatively, this
could be done the night before.
two Heat a large nonstick pan and add the
chicken and the marinade. Mix well and
cook over a moderate heat, stirring
constantly, for 15 mins.
three To serve, stir in the chopped parsley.

black olive chicken rolls

preparation time **10 mins**
cooking time **20 mins**
total time **30 mins** serves **4**

3 garlic cloves, crushed
2 tablespoons capers
4 anchovy fillets, chopped
1 teaspoon thyme leaves
1 shallot, chopped
175 g/6 oz pitted black olives
1 tablespoon olive oil, plus extra for oiling
4 small boneless, skinless chicken breasts
salt and pepper
cooked pasta, tossed in olive oil, chopped flat
    leaf parsley and grated Parmesan cheese,
    to serve

one Put the garlic, capers, anchovies,
thyme, shallot, olives and oil into a food
processor or blender and whizz together.
two Place each chicken breast between
2 sheets of greaseproof paper and flatten to
about 2½ times its original size by pounding
with a rolling pin. Season the chicken
breasts with salt and pepper and spread
each one with a thin layer of the olive paste.
three Roll up the breasts and secure with
2 wooden cocktail sticks. Cut each chicken
roll in half and place in a lightly oiled
ovenproof dish.
four Cover with foil and cook in the top of a
preheated oven, 200°C (400°F), Gas Mark 6,
for 20 mins or until cooked. Serve with
pasta tossed in oil, parsley and Parmesan.

chicken stuffed with spinach and ricotta

preparation time **5 mins**
cooking time **25 mins**
total time **30 mins** serves **4**

4 boneless, skinless chicken breasts
125 g/4 oz ricotta cheese
125 g/4 oz cooked spinach, squeezed dry
¼ teaspoon grated nutmeg
8 slices of Parma ham
2 tablespoons olive oil
salt and pepper

one Make a long horizontal slit through the
thickness of each chicken breast without
cutting right through.
two Crumble the ricotta into a bowl. Chop
the spinach and add to the ricotta with the
nutmeg. Season with salt and pepper and
mix well.
three Divide the stuffing between the
4 chicken breasts and wrap each one in
2 pieces of Parma ham, winding it around
the chicken to totally cover the meat.
four Heat the oil in a shallow, ovenproof
pan, add the chicken breasts and sauté for
4 mins on each side or until the ham starts
to brown. Transfer the pan to a preheated
oven, 200°C (400°F), Gas Mark 6, and cook
for 15 mins. The ham should be browned
and slightly crunchy on the outside and the
chicken moist and soft.

rolled stuffed chicken breasts

preparation time **10 mins**
cooking time **20 mins**
total time **30 mins** serves **4**

4 boneless, skinless chicken breasts
4 slices of Parma ham
4 thin slices of buffalo mozzarella
4 asparagus tips, plus extra to serve
75 g/3 oz plain flour
1 tablespoon olive oil
50 g/2 oz butter
50 ml/2 fl oz dry white wine
75 ml/3 fl oz chicken stock
salt and pepper

one Place each chicken breast between 2 sheets of greaseproof paper and flatten to about 2½ times its original size by pounding with a rolling pin.

two Season the chicken with salt and pepper, place a slice of Parma ham, a slice of mozzarella and an asparagus tip on top and tightly roll up the chicken breasts. Tie with a piece of strong thread or spear with wooden cocktail sticks.

three Season the flour with salt and pepper. Dip the prepared chicken rolls into the flour to coat evenly.

four Heat the oil and half of the butter in a frying pan, add the chicken rolls and sauté over a low heat for 15 mins or until golden all over, turning frequently to brown the chicken evenly.

five Remove the chicken, place in a warmed serving dish and keep warm. Pour the wine and stock into the pan, bring to the boil and simmer for 3 mins.

six Remove the thread or cocktail sticks just before serving the chicken. Add the remaining butter to the pan, mix quickly with a small whisk to emulsify the sauce, then spoon over the chicken and serve with steamed asparagus.

duck breasts with balsamic vinegar

preparation time **5 mins**
cooking time **25 mins**
total time **30 mins** serves **4**

1 tablespoon oil
4 boneless duck breasts
4 tablespoons balsamic vinegar
75 g/3 oz cranberries
50 g/2 oz brown sugar
salt and pepper

one Heat the oil in a frying pan, add the duck breasts, skin side down, and cook over a moderate heat for 5 mins. Reduce the heat and cook for another 10 mins. Drain the excess oil from the duck skin.

two Turn the duck breasts over and add the balsamic vinegar along with the cranberries and sugar. Season with salt and pepper and cook for a further 10 mins.

three Serve the cooked duck breasts with the sauce spooned over. The cranberries will have broken down and made a delicious sauce with the vinegar and juices from the duck. The duck breasts should remain pink and juicy in the middle.

grilled guinea fowl with fresh herb sauce

preparation time **10 mins**
cooking time **20 mins**
total time **30 mins** serves **4**

4 boneless guinea fowl breasts
2 tablespoons olive oil
salt and pepper

HERB SAUCE
3 garlic cloves, crushed
4 anchovy fillets, chopped
large handful of flat leaf parsley
handful of rocket leaves
handful of sorrel leaves
handful of basil leaves
juice of ½ lemon
125 ml/4 fl oz extra virgin olive oil

one Put the guinea fowl breasts, skin side up, on a lightly oiled grill pan, brush with a little oil and season with salt and pepper. Place the pan under a preheated hot grill and cook the guinea fowl for about 10 mins on each side.

two Meanwhile, make the herb sauce. Put the garlic, anchovies, parsley, rocket, sorrel, basil and lemon juice into a food processor or blender and whizz for 1 min. With the motor running, slowly drizzle in the oil; the sauce should be thick and bright green with a strong, fresh aroma. Finally, season with salt and pepper and blend again.

three The guinea fowl is ready when the skin is crunchy and dark brown. Serve with a little herb sauce on each plate and the remainder at the table in a small dish.

braised breast of wood pigeon

preparation time **5 mins**
cooking time **20 mins**
total time **25 mins** serves **4**

75 g/3 oz plain flour
8 wood pigeon breasts, skinned
2 tablespoons olive oil
1 red onion, chopped
2 garlic cloves, crushed
3 celery sticks, chopped
250 ml/8 fl oz red wine
grated rind of 1 orange
1 thyme sprig
1 rosemary sprig
1 bay leaf
½ teaspoon ground cinnamon
2 teaspoons juniper berries, crushed
200 g/7 oz redcurrant jelly
handful of flat leaf parsley, chopped
salt and pepper

one Season the flour with salt and pepper.
Dip the pigeon into the flour to coat
evenly.
two Heat the oil in a wide saucepan, add
the pigeon and cook for 2 mins on each
side. Remove from the pan.
three Add the onion, garlic and celery and
sauté for 5 mins. Increase the heat and
pour in the wine, stirring well.
four Add the orange rind, thyme, rosemary,
bay leaf, cinnamon, juniper berries,
redcurrant jelly and salt and pepper to taste.
Return the pigeon to the pan and baste well
with the sauce. Simmer for 10 mins.
five Remove the pigeon from the pan and
keep warm. Increase the heat and reduce
the liquid to a rich glaze. Return the
pigeon, add the parsley and serve.

quail with artichoke hearts

preparation time **5 mins**
cooking time **25 mins**
total time **30 mins** serves 4

75 g/3 oz plain flour
4 x 250 g/8 oz prepared quails
2 tablespoons olive oil
1 onion, chopped
2 celery sticks, chopped
2 garlic cloves, crushed
300 ml/½ pint white wine
handful of sage, chopped
400 g/13 oz jar artichoke hearts
salt and pepper
buttered pasta, to serve

one Sprinkle the flour on a plate and season
with salt and pepper. Dip the quail into the
flour to coat evenly.
two Heat the oil in a large saucepan, add
the quail and brown all over. Remove from
the pan and keep warm.
three Add the onion, celery and garlic and
sauté for 3 mins, then pour in the wine,
scraping any browned bits from the bottom
of the pan.
four Return the quail to the pan with the
sage and artichoke hearts and season well.
Cover the pan and simmer for 20 mins,
turning the quail from time to time. Serve
with buttered pasta.

Serve the rabbit on a bed of pappardelle,
if liked. Pappardelle is the traditional
pasta to be served with game.

sweet and sour rabbit

preparation time **5 mins**
cooking time **25 mins**
total time **30 mins** serves **4**

75 g/3 oz plain flour
1 rabbit, cut into 8 pieces
2 tablespoons olive oil
1 onion, diced
1 garlic clove, crushed
300 ml/½ pint red wine
1 rosemary sprig
4 tablespoons balsamic vinegar
1 tablespoon brown sugar
2 tablespoons sultanas
2 tablespoons pine nuts, toasted
2 tablespoons black olives, pitted and roughly
   chopped
salt and pepper

one Season the flour with salt and pepper.
Dip the rabbit into the flour to coat evenly.
two Heat the oil in a large frying pan, add
the rabbit pieces, turning to brown them all
over, then remove with a slotted spoon and
set aside.
three Add the onion and garlic and sauté
gently for 5 mins; do not brown.
four Return the rabbit to the pan, pour in
the wine and add the rosemary, vinegar,
sugar and sultanas. Season with salt and
pepper. Simmer for 20 mins, turning the
rabbit frequently to coat it in the sauce and
to cook evenly.
five Just before serving, add the pine nuts
and olives and stir to mix well.

pan-cooked rabbit with sage

preparation time **5 mins**
cooking time **25 mins**
total time **30 mins** serves **4**

2 tablespoons olive oil
1 rabbit, cut into 8 pieces
handful of chopped sage
1 large rosemary sprig
150 ml/¼ pint dry white wine
1 tablespoon Dijon mustard
salt and pepper
handful of flat leaf parsley, roughly chopped,
   to serve

one Heat the oil in a large frying pan, add
the rabbit and brown all over.
two Season well with salt and pepper.
Add the sage, rosemary, wine and mustard,
mix thoroughly and coat the rabbit in the
wine sauce.
three Simmer the rabbit for 20 mins, turning
frequently so that it cooks evenly.
four To serve, sprinkle the rabbit generously
with the chopped parsley.

grilled fillet of venison

preparation time **10 mins**
cooking time **15 mins**
total time **25 mins** serves **4**

4 x 175 g/6 oz venison fillet steaks
2 tablespoons olive oil, plus extra for sautéeing
1 shallot, finely chopped
2 garlic cloves, crushed
250 ml/8 fl oz red wine
4 cloves
1 piece of cinnamon stick
pared rind of 1 orange
10 juniper berries, crushed
3 tablespoons redcurrant jelly
salt and pepper
buttered pasta or Creamed Polenta with
    Dolcelatte and Mascarpone (see page 54),
    to serve

one Brush the venison steaks with the oil
and season well with salt and pepper.
two Heat a little oil in a saucepan, add the
shallot and garlic and sauté for 3 mins. Add
the wine, cloves, cinnamon, orange rind,
juniper berries and redcurrant jelly and
simmer until it reduces to a rich sauce.
three While the sauce is cooking, place
the venison fillets on a grill rack and cook
under a preheated hot grill for 6 mins on
each side.
four To serve, strain the sauce and spoon
over the venison steaks. Serve with
buttered pasta or Creamed Polenta with
Dolcelatte and Mascarpone (see page 54).

roast pork fillet with rosemary and fennel

preparation time **5 mins**
cooking time **25 mins**
total time **30 mins** serves **4**

1 large rosemary sprig
3 garlic cloves, peeled
750 g/1½ lb pork fillet, trimmed
4 tablespoons olive oil
2 fennel bulbs, trimmed and cut into wedges,
    central core removed
150 ml/¼ pint white wine
75 g/3 oz mascarpone cheese
salt and pepper
rosemary sprigs, to garnish

one Break the rosemary into short lengths
and cut the garlic into slices. Pierce the
pork with a sharp knife and insert the
pieces of rosemary and garlic evenly all
over the fillet.
two Heat half of the oil in a frying pan, add
the pork and fry for 5 mins or until browned
all over.
three Lightly oil a roasting tin, add the
fennel and drizzle with the remaining oil.
Place the pork on top, season generously
and roast in a preheated oven, 230°C
(450°F), Gas Mark 8, for 20 mins.
four Pour the wine into the frying pan
and simmer until reduced by half. Stir
in the mascarpone and salt and pepper
to taste.
five To serve, cut the pork into slices and
arrange on a warmed serving dish with
fennel wedges. Pour the sauce into the
roasting pan and place on the heat. Using
a wooden spoon, stir all the tasty bits into
the sauce, then spoon over the pork and
fennel. Garnish with rosemary sprigs.

Thin green beans simply cooked in boiling water
for 2 mins complement this rich and tasty dish.

parmesan breaded lamb chops

preparation time **10 mins**
cooking time **10 mins**
total time **20 mins** serves **4**

75 g/3 oz plain flour
8 lamb chops, trimmed
50 g/2 oz Parmesan cheese, freshly grated
50 g/2 oz fresh breadcrumbs
2 eggs, beaten
2 tablespoons olive oil
salt and pepper
1 lemon, cut into 4 wedges, to serve

one Season the flour with salt and pepper.
Dip the lamb chops into the flour to coat
evenly. Mix together the Parmesan and
breadcrumbs in a shallow dish and season
with salt and pepper.
two Dip the cutlets first into the beaten egg
and then into the Parmesan mixture to coat
all over, pressing the crumbs on to the lamb.
three Heat the oil in a frying pan, add the
lamb chops and cook on each side for
4 mins or until golden. Take care when
turning them over; a palette knife is best,
so as not to loosen any of the cheesy crust
from the chops.
four Serve immediately with lemon wedges.

fillet steak wrapped in parma ham

preparation time **10 mins**
cooking time **8 mins**
total time **18 mins** serves **4**

handful of chopped marjoram
2 garlic cloves, crushed
4 x 175 g/6 oz fillet steaks
8 slices of Parma ham
125 g/4 oz buffalo mozzarella, cut into
    4 slices
salt and pepper

one Mix together the marjoram and garlic
and season with salt and pepper. Coat the
steaks with the herb mixture, then wrap
them in the Parma ham. Make sure that all
the steak is covered with the ham.
two Put the steaks on a greased grill rack
and place under a preheated very hot grill,
as close to the heat as possible without
burning them. Cook for 3 mins on each side
if you like your steak rare, 5–6 mins for
medium and 8 mins for well done.
three Place the slices of mozzarella on
the steaks, return to the grill and cook until
the mozzarella is melting and just turning
golden.
four Remove the steaks from the grill and
leave to rest for 5 mins before serving. This
allows the meat to relax.

breaded veal escalopes with parma ham and parmesan

preparation time **10 mins**
cooking time **10 mins**
total time **20 mins** serves **4**

4 x 175 g/6 oz veal escalopes
75 g/3 oz plain flour
2 eggs, beaten
175 g/6 oz fresh breadcrumbs
75 g/3 oz butter
50 g/2 oz Parma ham
50 g/2 oz Parmesan cheese, freshly grated
salt and pepper
handful of flat leaf parsley, to garnish
1 lemon, cut into 4 wedges, to serve

one Place the veal escalopes between
2 sheets of greaseproof paper and flatten
them by pounding with a rolling pin.
two Season the flour with salt and pepper.
Dip the escalopes first into the flour, then
into the beaten egg and finally into the
breadcrumbs to coat evenly.
three Melt the butter in a large frying pan.
When it is foaming, add the escalopes and
cook for 1–2 mins on each side until golden.
four Place the escalopes on a grill pan. Put a
piece of Parma ham on each one and sprinkle
with grated Parmesan. Place the escalopes
under a preheated very hot grill and cook for
4–5 mins until the Parmesan is golden.
five Garnish the escalopes with chopped
parsley and serve with lemon wedges.

veal escalopes with lemon and pine nuts

preparation time **10 mins**
cooking time **10 mins**
total time **20 mins** serves **4**

75 g/3 oz plain flour
4 x 175 g/6 oz veal escalopes
50 g/2 oz butter
1 tablespoon olive oil
75 g/3 oz pine nuts
rind and juice of 1 lemon
75 ml/3 fl oz chicken stock
handful of parsley, finely chopped
salt and pepper
Risotto alla Milanese (see page 40), to serve

one Season the flour with salt and pepper.
Dip the veal escalopes into the flour to
coat evenly.
two Heat the butter and oil in a frying pan.
When it is foaming, add the escalopes and
cook for 3 mins on each side or until golden.
three Sprinkle the pine nuts into the pan
and stir until golden.
four Add the lemon rind and juice, stock and
parsley and season with salt and pepper.
Bring to the boil and mix well. Serve
immediately with Risotto alla Milanese (see
page 40).

It is important that all the ingredients for the
gremolata are finely chopped or grated as they
mix together better, making a more subtle blend.

veal chops with gremolata

preparation time **5 mins**
cooking time **25 mins**
total time **30 mins** serves **4**

4 thin veal chops
75 g/3 oz seasoned flour
50 g/2 oz butter
1 tablespoon olive oil
2 onions, chopped
2 garlic cloves, crushed
2 celery sticks, chopped
1 carrot, chopped
2 bay leaves
6 tomatoes, skinned, deseeded and chopped
125 ml/4 fl oz chicken stock
125 ml/4 fl oz dry white wine
salt and pepper

GREMOLATA
2 tablespoons finely chopped parsley
1 tablespoon finely chopped sage
rind of 3 lemons, finely grated
3 large garlic cloves, crushed

one Coat both sides of the veal chops with seasoned flour. Melt the butter with the oil in a flameproof casserole, add the chops and brown well on each side. Remove from the casserole and keep warm.

two Add the onions, garlic, celery and carrot to the pan and sauté for 3 mins.

three Add the bay leaves, tomatoes, stock, wine and salt and pepper to taste, mix well and bring to the boil. Return the chops to the casserole and turn to coat them in the sauce. Cover and cook in a preheated oven, 200°C (400°F), Gas Mark 6, for 20 mins.

four While the chops are cooking, make the gremolata. Mix together all the ingredients in a bowl.

five To serve, transfer the chops to a warmed serving plate and keep them warm. Boil the sauce to reduce if necessary, then pour it over the chops and spoon some of the gremolata over each one.

desserts

This chapter includes some classic Italian desserts as well as some unusual new ideas including sweet and chocolate risottos.

zabaglione

preparation time **5 mins**
cooking time **10 mins**
total time **15 mins** serves **4**

4 egg yolks
75 g/3 oz caster sugar, plus extra for frosting
    the glasses
grated rind of ½ lemon
½ teaspoon ground cinnamon, plus extra
    to decorate
1 drop of vanilla extract
150 ml/¼ pint Marsala
125 g/4 oz fresh fruit (such as peaches, apricots
    and berries), sliced

one Place the egg yolks, caster sugar,
lemon rind, cinnamon and vanilla extract in
a heatproof bowl and beat with an electric
whisk until thick, pale and creamy.
two Place the bowl over a saucepan of
simmering water and continue whisking.
Slowly add the Marsala and whisk until the
mixture is warm, frothy and thick.
three To serve, dip the rims of 4 glasses in
water, then in sugar to frost them. Divide
the fruit between the glasses, then spoon in
the zabaglione. Dust with a little extra
cinnamon before serving.

This dish is best made the night
before so that it can set completely.

tiramisu with raspberry surprise

preparation time **15 mins**, plus chilling
total time **15 mins** serves **4**

4 tablespoons very strong espresso coffee
2 tablespoons grappa or brandy
10 sponge fingers
125 g/4 oz raspberries
175 g/6 oz mascarpone cheese
2 eggs, separated
50 g/2 oz icing sugar
25 g/1 oz dark chocolate

one Combine the coffee and grappa or
brandy in a bowl. Dip the sponge fingers
into the liquid to coat evenly, then arrange
them on a small shallow dish or a serving
platter, pouring over any excess liquid.
Sprinkle the raspberries evenly over the
soaked sponge fingers.
two Whisk the mascarpone, egg yolks and
icing sugar together in a bowl until smooth
and well blended.
three In a separate bowl, whisk the egg
whites until stiff and glossy, then fold the
egg whites and the mascarpone mixture
together until well blended.
four Spoon the mixture over the sponge
fingers and smooth the surface. Finely grate
the chocolate straight on to the mixture.
Cover and chill until set.

This dessert is very good if made the night before to allow all the flavours to blend together.

italian trifle

preparation time **10 mins**
cooking time **10 mins**
total time **20 mins** serves **4**

8 sponge fingers
2 tablespoons blueberry jam
50 ml/2 fl oz Marsala or sherry
250 g/8 oz blueberries
300 ml/½ pint milk
1 tablespoon cornflour
2 egg yolks
2 tablespoons sugar
300 ml/½ pint whipping cream
50 g/2 oz chocolate, grated

one Spread the sponge fingers with the jam and arrange in a glass serving bowl. Sprinkle over the Marsala or sherry and add half of the blueberries.

two Mix a little milk with the cornflour to make a smooth paste. Stir the paste into the remainder of the milk. Pour into a saucepan and bring to the boil, stirring constantly as the milk will thicken. When it is boiling and smooth, remove it from the heat.

three Whisk the egg yolks and sugar together in a large bowl until they are light and creamy. Add the thickened milk to the beaten egg mixture, whisking constantly. Blend well and pour over the blueberries, then top with the remaining blueberries. Allow to cool.

four Softly whip the cream and spread over the trifle, then top with the grated chocolate.

blood orange granita

preparation time **10 mins**, plus freezing
total time **10 mins** serves **4**

1 kg/2 lb blood oranges
250 g/8 oz sugar

one Using a sharp knife, cut off the top and bottom of the oranges, then cut away the pith and peel. Working over a bowl to catch the juice, cut the segments out of the oranges and squeeze any excess juice from each one.

two Strain the juice into a saucepan, add the sugar and heat until it has dissolved.

three Place the orange flesh in a food processor or blender and whizz until smooth. Mix in the juice and pour into ice cube trays to freeze.

four When you serve the granita, first chill the serving dishes for a short while in the freezer. To serve, remove the granita ice cubes from the freezer, put them into the food processor or blender and whizz for 30 seconds, then transfer them to the serving dishes and serve immediately.

caramelized orange and pineapple

preparation time **10 mins**
cooking time **10 mins**
total time **20 mins** serves **4**

4 oranges
175 g/6 oz sugar
125 ml/4 fl oz water
1 small pineapple

one With a very sharp knife, remove the rind from 2 of the oranges and slice it into very fine strips. Place the rind in a saucepan of boiling water and simmer for 2 mins. Remove and drain well.

two Put the sugar and water into a saucepan and heat gently, swishing the pan constantly until the sugar is dissolved. Increase the heat and boil the syrup until it turns a golden brown. Take care not to overcook the caramel – if it gets too dark, carefully add 2 tablespoons of water. Stand back when adding the water as the caramel spits. Set aside when ready.

three To peel the oranges, cut a slice off the top and bottom of each one, then place the orange on one of these cut sides and take a knife around the side of the orange, cutting away the skin and pith. Cut across the orange into about 6–7 slices.

four To prepare the pineapple, top and tail it and slice away the skin from top to bottom. Make sure that you remove the 'eyes' close to the skin. Cut the pineapple into quarters and remove the core. Cut into slices.

five Make alternate layers of orange and pineapple in a heatproof dish. Sprinkle with the orange rind, pour over the caramel and leave to stand until required.

panettone pudding

preparation time **5 mins**
cooking time **25 mins**
total time **30 mins** serves **4**

50 g/2 oz butter
5 slices of panettone
a little apricot jam, for spreading
250 ml/8 fl oz milk
250 ml/8 fl oz double cream
2 eggs
1 egg yolk
50 g/2 oz brown sugar, plus extra for the crust

one Butter a 1.2 litre/2 pint ovenproof dish. Spread the panettone slices with the apricot jam and cut them into triangles or rectangles. Place in the buttered dish; try and arrange them in overlapping layers.

two Put the milk and cream into a saucepan and bring gently to the boil.

three Whisk together the eggs, egg yolk and sugar in a bowl until creamy and fluffy. Continue whisking and slowly add the hot milk and cream. When it is all combined, carefully pour it over the panettone; make sure that it is all covered by the custard mixture. Sprinkle with a little extra sugar to make a nice crunchy crust.

four Fill a roasting tin with boiling water, place the panettone pudding in the bain marie and bake in a preheated oven, 180°C (350°F), Gas Mark 4, for 25 mins or until the custard is set.

This dish is very good if prepared up to the cooking stage the night before and then kept in the refrigerator. This allows the panettone to soak up the custard.

lemon polenta syrup cake

preparation time **5 mins**
cooking time **25 mins**
total time **30 mins** serves **4–6**

175 g/6 oz butter
175 g/6 oz caster sugar
125 g/4 oz ground almonds
50 g/2 oz flaked almonds
½ teaspoon vanilla extract
2 large eggs
finely grated rind and juice of 1 lemon
75 g/3 oz polenta flour
½ teaspoon baking powder
single cream, to serve

SYRUP
grated rind and juice of 2 lemons
50 g/2 oz caster sugar
2 tablespoons of water

one Line a 15 cm/6 inch cake tin with baking parchment.
two Beat together the butter and sugar in a bowl until light and creamy. Add the ground and flaked almonds, vanilla extract and eggs and mix well. Add the lemon rind and juice, polenta and baking powder and mix well. Spoon into the prepared tin and bake in a preheated oven, 180°C (350°F), Gas Mark 4, for 25 mins.
three While the cake is cooking, make the syrup. Put the lemon rind and juice, caster sugar and water into a saucepan and heat through. Spoon over the cake as soon as it comes out of the oven. Allow the syrup to drizzle through. Serve the cake hot or cold with single cream.

almond soufflés

preparation time **10 mins**
cooking time **12 mins**
total time **22 mins** serves **4**

15 g/½ oz butter, plus extra for greasing
25 g/1 oz plain flour, plus extra for dusting
200 ml/7 fl oz milk
75 g/3 oz ground almonds
3 eggs, separated
25 g/1 oz caster sugar
75 ml/3 fl oz Amaretto di Saronno
4 macaroons, crushed
icing sugar, to decorate

one Butter 4 small soufflé dishes and dust with flour.
two Melt the butter in a small saucepan, add the flour and stir to a smooth paste. Slowly pour in the milk, stirring constantly, to make a smooth sauce. Add the ground almonds and egg yolks and mix well and rapidly. Do not leave the pan on the heat. Add the caster sugar and the Amaretto and mix well again.
three Quickly whisk the egg whites in a large bowl until stiff. Fold in the almond sauce, then quickly fold in the crushed macaroons.
four Divide the mixture between the prepared soufflé dishes and cook in a preheated oven, 220°C (425°F), Gas Mark 7, for 12 mins or until risen and golden. Dust with icing sugar and serve immediately.

These macaroons are delicious served with coffee. They can be stored in an airtight container for up to 10 days.

almond macaroons

preparation time **10 mins**
cooking time **15 mins**
total time **25 mins** makes approximately **16**

125 g/4 oz ground almonds
150 g/5 oz caster sugar
2 large egg whites
½ teaspoon almond extract

one Line 3 baking sheets with baking parchment.

two Mix the ground almonds and sugar together thoroughly. Whisk the egg whites and almond extract in a large bowl until stiff and glossy. Add the ground almond mixture to the egg whites and fold in until evenly blended.

three Using a small teaspoon, place spoonfuls of the mixture on the baking sheets leaving space between them so that they can expand slightly. Place the baking sheets in a preheated oven, 180°C (350°F), Gas Mark 4, and bake for 15 mins. The macaroons should be golden and slightly firm to the touch.

four Remove the macaroons from the oven and leave for 5 mins to cool and set. Lift them off the baking parchment with a thin palette knife and leave to cool completely.

baked peaches with almonds and honey

preparation time **5 mins**
cooking time **15 mins**
total time **20 mins** serves **4**

50 g/2 oz butter, plus extra for greasing
4 large ripe peaches, halved and stoned
50 g/2 oz flaked almonds
4 tablespoons clear honey
a little ground cinnamon
crème fraîche, to serve

one Butter a shallow baking dish large enough to take 8 peach halves.

two Place the peaches in the baking dish, skin side down. Dot with butter, then sprinkle with the almonds, drizzle with the honey and dust with cinnamon.

three Bake the peaches at the top of a preheated oven, 200°C (400°F), Gas Mark 6, for 10–15 mins. You want to get a little colour into the peaches and allow the almonds to lightly brown.

four Serve the peaches with the juices drizzled over and topped with a spoonful of crème fraîche.

almond brittle

preparation time **5 mins**
cooking time **10 mins**
total time **15 mins** serves **8**

250 g/8 oz blanched almonds
250 g/8 oz sugar

one Line a baking tray with baking
parchment.
two Put the almonds on a grill pan and place
under a preheated grill until lightly brown.
Allow to cool a little, then roughly chop.
three Heat a nonstick frying pan over a
moderate heat, add the sugar and allow to
melt into caramel. Take care that the heat is
not too high or the caramel will burn and
have a very bitter taste. Add the almonds
and mix in, then pour the almond brittle into
the prepared baking tray.
four Leave the almond brittle to cool, then
break it into small pieces.

Serve this almond brittle with ice cream or
good strong coffee. Store it in an airtight
container.

poached pears with honey and cinnamon

preparation time **5 mins**
cooking time **20 mins**
total time **25 mins** serves **4**

rind and juice of 1 lemon
450 ml/¾ pint red wine
150 ml/5 fl oz water
5 tablespoons clear honey
1 mace blade
1 cinnamon stick
6 cloves
4 ripe pears, peeled
thick yogurt, to serve

one Put the lemon rind and juice, wine,
water, honey, mace, cinnamon and cloves
into a saucepan and bring to a gentle boil.
two Add the pears and simmer for 10 mins or
until they are soft, turning them occasionally.
three Remove the pears with a slotted
spoon and set aside. Transfer the liquid to
a saucepan with a larger surface area. Place
the pan over a high heat and boil the liquid
rapidly to make a rich, thick, sticky syrup.
Spoon the syrup over the pears and serve
with thick yogurt.

Serve the chocolate risotto in coffee cups for an Italian
flavour. Use a good-quality dark chocolate with a high
percentage of cocoa butter – at least 70%.

chocolate risotto

preparation time **5 mins**
cooking time **20 mins**
total time **25 mins** serves **4**

600 ml/1 pint milk
25 g/1 oz sugar
50 g/2 oz butter
125 g/4 oz arborio or carnaroli rice
50 g/2 oz hazelnuts, toasted and chopped
50 g/2 oz sultanas
125 g/4 oz good-quality dark chocolate, grated
splash of brandy (optional)
grated chocolate, to decorate

one Put the milk and sugar into a saucepan and heat to simmering point.
two Melt the butter in a heavy-based saucepan, add the rice and stir well to coat the grains.
three Add a ladleful of hot milk and stir well. When the rice has absorbed the milk, add another ladleful. Continue to add the milk in stages and stir until it is all absorbed. The rice should be slightly *al dente* and with a creamy sauce.
four Finally, add the hazelnuts, sultanas and grated chocolate and mix quickly. Serve decorated with a little grated chocolate. Try not to overmix the chocolate as the marbled effect looks good. For a special treat, add a splash of brandy just before decorating and serving the risotto.

sweet risotto

preparation time **5 mins**
cooking time **20 mins**
total time **25 mins** serves **4**

600 ml/1 pint milk
25 g/1 oz sugar
½ teaspoon vanilla extract
50 g/2 oz butter
finely grated rind of 1 lemon
125 g/4 oz arborio or carnaroli rice
50 g/2 oz raisins
50 g/2 oz toasted flaked almonds
3 tablespoons honey

one Put the milk, sugar and vanilla extract into a saucepan and heat to simmering point, then turn off the heat.
two Melt the butter in a heavy-based saucepan, add the lemon rind and rice and mix well to coat the grains.
three Add the raisins and a ladleful of hot milk and stir well. When the rice has absorbed the milk, add another ladleful. Continue to add the milk in stages and stir until it is all absorbed. The rice should be slightly *al dente* and with a creamy sauce.
four Serve the risotto in individual dishes, sprinkled with toasted flaked almonds and drizzled with honey.

This unusual sweet risotto is not unlike a creamy rice pudding, but with more flavour.

Index

almonds: almond brittle, 123
almond macaroons, 122
almond soufflès, 119
baked peaches with almonds and honey, 122
anchovies: anchovy and red pepper pizza, 53
broccoli with anchovies, 81
Sicilian aubergines, 81
artichokes: artichoke and goats' cheese pizza, 51
quail with artichoke hearts, 105
asparagus, penne with broad beans, mint and, 29
aubergines: aubergine salad, 69
aubergine, tomato and mozzarella mountains, 66–7
baked aubergine and Gorgonzola, 80
caponata, 66
Sicilian aubergines, 81
stuffed aubergines, 80

bacon: spaghetti carbonara, 35
balsamic vinegar, 9
balsamic braised leeks and peppers, 76–7
duck breasts with balsamic vinegar, 104
basil, 10
bay leaves, 10
beans: rocket, tuna and haricot bean salad, 70
Tuscan bean soup, 19
white bean and sun-dried tomato salad, 65
beef: fillet steak wrapped in Parma ham, 110
blood orange granita, 117
blueberries: Italian trifle, 117
borlotti beans: Tuscan bean soup, 19
bread: bruschetta, 20
crostini, 20–1
panzanella, 62

broad beans: braised broad beans and lentils, 85
penne with broad beans, asparagus and mint, 29
broccoli: broccoli with anchovies, 81
spinach and broccoli soup, 14
bruschetta, 20
butternut squashes, 11
butternut squash risotto, 44
butternut squash soup, 17

Caesar salad, 62–3
capers, 9
caponata, 66
caramelized orange and pineapple, 118
cavolo nero, 9
cavolo nero with pancetta, 84–5
celery: baked young celery with Parmesan, 79
cheese, 9
artichoke and goats' cheese pizza, 51
aubergine, tomato and mozzarella mountains, 66–7
baked aubergine and Gorgonzola, 80
baked polenta with fontina, 57
baked young celery with Parmesan, 79
breaded veal escalopes with Parma ham and Parmesan, 111
chicken and Parmesan salad, 70
chicken stuffed with spinach and ricotta, 102
classic tomato pizza, 50
crostini, 20–1
fennel baked with cream and Parmesan, 78
fusilli with Parmesan and pine nuts, 27

mushroom and mozzarella lasagne stacks, 30–1
Parmesan breaded lamb chops, 110
pasta bake with spinach and ham, 36–7
rich polenta salad, 58–9
rolled stuffed chicken breasts, 103
spinach and ricotta frittata, 78
stuffed aubergines, 80
trout with Parmesan and basil dressing, 90
chicken: black olive chicken rolls, 102
chicken and Parmesan salad, 70
chicken stuffed with spinach and ricotta, 102
chicken with rosemary and garlic, 101
country chicken, 100
rolled stuffed chicken breasts, 103
Roman chicken, 101
chicken livers: chicken livers with Marsala and oregano, 100
penne with, 35
chillies, pan-fried squid with, 96–7
chocolate, 9
chocolate risotto, 125
ciabatta, 9
clams: fish casserole, 92
spaghetti vongole, 32
cod: roast cod with vegetables, 95
coffee: tiramisu with raspberry surprise, 116
courgettes: courgette fritters, 75
fried courgettes with chillies, 75
crab sauce, tagliatelle with, 33
crostini, 20–1

duck breasts with balsamic vinegar, 104

eggs: spaghetti carbonara, 35
spinach and ricotta frittata, 78
spinach, Parma ham and egg pizza, 54
vegetable frittata, 76

farfalle, 10
saffron bows, 26
fennel, 9
fennel baked with cream and Parmesan, 78
roast pork fillet with rosemary and fennel, 108
figs with Parma ham, 71
fillet steak wrapped in Parma ham, 110
fish and shellfish, 87–97
fish casserole, 92
focaccia, 9
frittata: spinach and ricotta frittata, 78
vegetable frittata, 76
fritters, courgette, 75
fruit: zabaglione, 116
fusilli, 10
with Parmesan and pine nuts, 27

garlic, 9
granita, blood orange, 117
green beans: tomato and green bean salad, 65
gremolata, veal chops with, 113
guinea fowl grilled with fresh herb sauce, 104

halibut in paper parcels, 93
ham: pasta bake with spinach and ham, 36–7
see also Parma ham
haricot bean, rocket and tuna salad, 70
herbs, 10
green herb risotto, 44

Italian trifle, 117

lamb chops, Parmesan breaded, 110

lasagne, 10
  mushroom and
    mozzarella lasagne
    stacks, 30–1
leeks: balsamic braised
  leeks and peppers, 76–7
lemon: lemon and basil
  orzo, 29
  lemon polenta syrup
  cake, 119
lentils, 11
  braised broad beans
    and lentils, 85
linguine, 10
  with vegetables, 24–5
lobster, spaghetti with, 33

macaroons, almond, 122
Marsala: chicken livers
  with Marsala and
  oregano, 100
zabaglione, 116
mascarpone, 9
  creamed polenta with
    Dolcelatte and
    mascarpone, 54–5
  tiramisu with raspberry
    surprise, 116
melon and Parma ham
  soup, 14
minestrone soup, 16
monkfish: roast monkfish
  with Parma ham, 93
mushrooms, 11
  fresh wild mushroom
    pizza, 51
  grilled polenta with
    mushrooms and
    Parma ham, 58
  mushroom and
    mozzarella lasagne
    stacks, 30–1
  pappardelle with
    prosciutto and porcini,
    34
  red wine risotto, 43
  risotto with forest
    mushrooms and sage,
    42–3
mussels: fish casserole,
  92
  mussel soup, 19
  mussels with fresh
    tomato and pepper
    sauce, 95

olive oil, 10
olives, 10

black olive chicken rolls,
  102
crostini, 20–1
pappardelle with olives
  and capers, 27
oranges: blood orange
  granita, 117
  caramelized orange and
    pineapple, 118
orecchiette, 10
  with spicy tomato and
    pancetta sauce, 36
oregano, 10
orzo, 10
  lemon and basil orzo,
  29

pancetta, 10
  cavolo nero with
    pancetta, 84–5
  orecchiette with spicy
    tomato and pancetta
    sauce, 36
panettone, 10
  panettone pudding,
    118–19
panzanella, 62
pappardelle, 10
  with olives and capers,
    27
  with prosciutto and
    porcini, 34
Parma ham, 10
  breaded veal escalopes
    with Parma ham and
    Parmesan, 111
  figs with Parma ham,
    71
  fillet steak wrapped in
    Parma ham, 110
  grilled polenta with
    mushrooms and
    Parma ham, 58
  melon and Parma ham
    soup, 14
  potatoes wrapped in
    Parma ham, 82–3
  roast monkfish with
    Parma ham, 93
  rolled stuffed chicken
    breasts, 103
  spinach, Parma ham
    and egg pizza, 54
Parmesan breaded lamb
  chops, 110
pasta, 10, 23–37
pasta bake with spinach
  and ham, 36–7

pasta primavera, 24
peaches, baked with
  almonds and honey, 122
pears, poached with
  honey and cinnamon,
  123
penne, 10
  with broad beans,
    asparagus and mint,
    29
  with chicken livers, 35
  with tomato and chilli,
    26
peppers: anchovy and red
  pepper pizza, 53
  balsamic braised leeks
    and peppers, 76–7
  crostini, 20–1
  mushroom and
    mozzarella lasagne
    stacks, 30–1
  mussels with fresh
    tomato and pepper
    sauce, 95
  Piedmont peppers, 69
  Sicilian aubergines, 81
pesto and green
  vegetable soup, 16
Piedmont peppers, 69
pine nuts, 11
  fusilli with Parmesan
    and pine nuts, 27
pineapple, caramelized
  orange and, 118
pizzas, 49–54
  anchovy and red pepper
    pizza, 53
  artichoke and goats'
    cheese pizza, 51
  classic tomato pizza, 50
  fresh vegetable pizza,
    53
  fresh wild mushroom
    pizza, 51
  quick pizza base, 50
  spinach, Parma ham
    and egg pizza, 54
polenta, 11
  baked polenta with
    fontina, 57
  creamed polenta with
    Dolcelatte and
    mascarpone, 54–5
  grilled polenta with
    mushrooms and
    Parma ham, 58
  lemon polenta syrup
    cake, 119

rich polenta salad, 58–9
pork: roast pork fillet with
  rosemary and fennel,
  108
potatoes: potatoes
  wrapped in Parma ham,
  82–3
  roast potatoes with
    rosemary and garlic, 83
prawns: fish casserole, 92
  tiger prawns with garlic
    and herbs, 96
prosciutto, pappardelle
  with porcini and, 34
pumpkin seed oil, 11
Puy lentils, 11

quail with artichoke
  hearts, 105

rabbit: pan-cooked rabbit
  with sage, 107
  sweet and sour rabbit,
    107
raspberry surprise,
  tiramisu with, 116
red mullet: fish
  casserole, 92
  grilled red mullet with
    salsa verde, 90–1
rice, 11
  see also risotto
risotto, 39–47
  butternut squash
    risotto, 44
  chocolate risotto, 125
  green herb risotto, 44
  green risotto, 40
  red wine risotto, 43
  risotto alla Milanese, 40
  risotto with forest
    mushrooms and sage,
    42–3
  seafood risotto, 46
  spinach and lemon
    risotto, 46
  sweet risotto, 125
rocket, tuna and haricot
  bean salad, 70
Roman chicken, 101
rosemary, 10

saffron, 11
  saffron bows, 26
salads, 61–71
  aubergine salad, 69
  Caesar salad, 62–3
  caponata, 66

chicken and Parmesan salad, 70
panzanella, 62
Piedmont peppers, 69
rich polenta salad, 58–9
rocket, tuna and haricot bean salad, 70
tomato and green bean salad, 65
white bean and sun-dried tomato salad, 65
salsa verde, grilled red mullet with, 90–1
salt, 11
sardines, spicy fried, 89
sea bass, grilled, 88
seafood risotto, 46
shellfish and fish, 87–97
Sicilian aubergines, 81
soufflès, almond, 119
soups, 13–19
  butternut squash soup, 17
  melon and Parma ham soup, 14
  minestrone soup, 16
  mussel soup, 19
  pesto and green vegetable soup, 16
  spinach and broccoli soup, 14
  Tuscan bean soup, 19
spaghetti, 10
  spaghetti carbonara, 35
  spaghetti vongole, 32
  spaghetti with lobster, 33
spinach: chicken stuffed with spinach and ricotta, 102
  pasta bake with spinach and ham, 36–7

quick spinach, 74
spinach and broccoli soup, 14
spinach and lemon risotto, 46
spinach and ricotta frittata, 78
spinach, Parma ham and egg pizza, 54
squashes, 11
  butternut squash risotto, 44
  butternut squash soup, 17
squid: fish casserole, 92
  pan-fried squid with chillies, 96–7
sweet and sour rabbit, 107
swordfish steaks in white wine and tomatoes, 88

tagliatelle, 10
  with crab sauce, 33
tiger prawns with garlic and herbs, 96
tiramisu with raspberry surprise, 116
tomatoes, 11
  aubergine, tomato and mozzarella mountains, 66–7
  baked aubergine and Gorgonzola, 80
  baked polenta with fontina, 57
  classic tomato pizza, 50
  mussels with fresh tomato and pepper sauce, 95
  orecchiette with spicy

tomato and pancetta sauce, 36
penne with tomato and chilli, 26
swordfish steaks in white wine and tomatoes, 88
tomato and green bean salad, 65
tuna steaks with sun-dried tomatoes, 89
white bean and sun-dried tomato salad, 65
tortellini, 10
trifle, Italian, 117
trout with Parmesan and basil dressing, 90
truffle oil, 11
truffles, 11
tuna: rocket, tuna and haricot bean salad, 70
  tuna steaks with sun-dried tomatoes, 89
Tuscan bean soup, 19

veal: breaded veal escalopes with Parma ham and Parmesan, 111
veal chops with gremolata, 113
veal escalopes with lemon and pine nuts, 111
vegetables: fresh vegetable pizza, 53
  green risotto, 40
  linguine with vegetables, 24–5
  pasta primavera, 24
  pesto and green vegetable soup, 16

roast cod with vegetables, 95
roast vegetables with olive oil and chillies, 79
vegetable frittata, 76
venison, grilled fillet of, 108
vinegar, balsamic, 9

white bean and sun-dried tomato salad, 65
wine: red wine risotto, 43
wood pigeon, braised breast of, 105

zabaglione, 116

Acknowledgements

Executive Editor: Sarah Ford
Project Editor: Jessica Cowie
Executive Art Editor: Geoff Fennell
Designer: Sue Michniewicz

Photographer: David Loftus
Stylist: Wei Tang
Home Economist: Fran Warde
Production Controller: Ian Paton

BELIEVE IN
YOURSELF

By

JOSEPH MURPHY

D.D. Ph.D., LL.D.

Martino Publishing
Mansfield Centre, CT
2010

Martino Publishing
P.O. Box 373,
Mansfield Centre, CT 06250 USA

www.martinopublishing.com

ISBN 978-1578989713

Cover design by T. Matarazzo

Printed in the United States of America On 100% Acid-Free Paper

BELIEVE IN YOURSELF

By

JOSEPH MURPHY
D.D. Ph.D., LL.D.

WILLING PUBLISHING COMPANY
P.O. Box 51
San Gabriel, California

CONTENTS

CHAPTER   PAGE

MAKE YOUR DREAMS COME TRUE 7

USING THE SUBCONSCIOUS MIND IN BUSINESS....41

HOW TO IMAGINE SUCCESS 69

MAKE YOUR DREAMS COME TRUE

*"Now Israel loved Joseph more than all his chil-
dren, because he was the son of his old age: and he
made him a coat of many colours.*

*"And when his brethren saw that their father loved
him more than all his brethren, they hated him, and
could not speak peaceably unto him.*

*"And Joseph dreamed a dream, and he told it his
brethren: and they hated him all the more.*

*"And he said unto them, Hear, I pray you, this
dream which I have dreamed:*

*"For, behold, we were binding sheaves in the field,
and, lo, my sheaf arose, and also stood upright; and,
behold, your sheaves stood round about, and made
obeisance to my sheaf.*

*"And his brethren said to him, Shalt thou indeed
reign over us? or shalt thou indeed have dominion
over us? And they hated him yet the more for his
dream, and for his words.*

*"And he dreamed yet another dream, and told it his
brethren, and said, Behold, I have dreamed a dream
more; and behold, the sun and the moon and the
eleven stars made obiesance to me.*

*"And he told it to his father, and his brethren:
and his father rebuked him, and said unto him, What
is this dream that thou hast dreamed? Shall I and
thy mother and thy brethren indeed come to bow
down to thee to the earth?"* (Genesis 37:3-10.)

7

BELIEVE IN YOURSELF

Joseph in the Bible means disciplined or controlled imagination. It is one of the primal faculties of mind, and has the power to project and clothe your ideas, giving them visibility on the screen of space.

Israel loved Joseph. *Israel* is the spiritually awakened man who knows the power of controlled imagination. It is called the son of his old age. *Son* means expression. *Old age* infers wisdom and knowledge of the laws of mind. When you become familiar with the power of imagination, you will call it "the son of your old age."

Age is not the flight of years; it is really the dawn of wisdom and Divine knowledge in you. *Imagination* is the mighty instrument used by great scientists, artists, physicists, inventors, architects, and mystics. When the world said, "It is impossible. It can't be done," the man with imagination said, "It *is* done!" Through your imagination you can also penetrate the depths of reality, and reveal the secrets of nature.

A great industrialist told me one time how he started in a small store. He said that I used to dream (Joseph was a dreamer) of a large corporation with branches all over the country. He added that regularly and systematically he pictured in his mind the giant building, offices, factories, and stores, knowing that through the alchemy of the mind, he could weave the fabric out of which his dreams would be clothed. He prospered, and began to attract to himself by a universal law of attraction the ideas, personnel, friends, money, and everything needed for the unfoldment of his ideal. He truly exercised and cultivated his imagination, and lived with these mental patterns in his mind until imagination clothed them in form.

I liked particularly one comment which he made as follows, "It is just as easy to imagine yourself successful, as it is to imagine failure, and far more interesting."

Joseph is a dreamer, and a dreamer of dreams; this means he has visions, images, and ideals in his mind, and knows that there is a Creative Power which responds to his mental pictures. The mental images we hold are developed in feeling. It is wisely said that all our senses are modifications of the one-sense-feeling. Troward says, "Feeling is the law, and the law is the feeling." Feeling is the fountain-head of power. We must charge

9

our mental pictures with feeling in order to get results.

We are told, "Joseph dreamed a dream, and told it to his brethren, and they hated him." Perhaps as you read this, you have a dream, an ideal, a plan, or purpose that you would like to accomplish. *To hate* is to reject in Bible language. The thoughts, feelings, beliefs, and opinions in your mind are your brethren which challenge you, belittle your dreams, and say to you, "You can't; it is impossible." "Forget it!" Perhaps other thoughts come into your mind which scoff at your plan or ambition. You discover there is a quarrel in your mind with your own brethren; opposition sets in. The way to handle the opposition in your mind is to detach your attention from sense evidence and appearance of things, and begin to think clearly and with interest about your goal or objective. When your mind is engaged on your goal or objective, you are using the creative law of mind, and it will come to pass.

"Lo, my sheaf arose, and also stood upright; and, behold, your sheaves stood round about, and made obeisance to my sheaf." Lift your ideal or desire up in consciousness. Exalt it. Commit yourself whole-heartedly to it. Praise it; give your at-

10

tention, love, and devotion to your ideal, and as
you continue to do this, all the fearful thoughts will
make obeisance to your exalted state of mind;
i.e., they will lose their power, and disappear from
the mind. Through your faculty to imagine the
end result, you have control over any circumstance
or condition. If you wish to bring about the realization of any wish, desire, or idea, form a mental
picture of fulfillment in your mind; constantly
imagine the reality of your desire. In this way you
will actually compel it into being. What you
imagine as true already exists in the next dimen-
sion of mind, and if you remain faithful to your
ideal, it will one day objectify itself. The master-
architect within you will project on the screen of
visibility what you impress on your mind.

Joseph (imagination) wears a coat of many
colors. A *coat* in the Bible is a psychological cov-
ering. Your psychological garments are the mental attitudes, moods, and feelings you entertain.
The coat of many colors represent the many facets
of the diamond, or your capacity to clothe any
idea in form. You can imagine your friend who
is poor living in the lap of luxury. You can see
his face light up with joy, see his expression
change, and a broad smile cross his lips. You can

11

hear him tell you what you want to hear. You can see him exactly as you wish to see him — i.e., he is radiant, happy, prosperous, and successful. Your imagination is the *coat of many colors;* it can clothe and objectify any idea or desire. You can imagine abundance where lack is; peace where discord is; health where sickness is.

"His brethren said to him, Shalt thou indeed reign over us?" Imagination is the first faculty, and takes precedence over all the other powers or elements of consciousness. You have twelve faculties or brethren, but your imagination when disciplined enables you to collapse time and space and rise above all limitations. When you keep your imagination busy with noble, God-like concepts and ideas, you will find it is the most effective of all faculties in your spiritual ongoing.

The phrase, "Joseph is sold into Egypt —" means that your concept or desire must be subjectified (Egypt) first before it becomes objectified. Every concept must go "down into Egypt"— meaning into the subjective where the birth of ideas takes place.

"Out of Egypt have I called my son—" Joseph is commander of Egypt which tells you that imagination controls the whole conceptive realm.

12

Whatever prison you may be in, whether it is the prison of fear, sickness, lack, or limitation of any kind, remember that Joseph is the commander in prison, and can deliver you. You can imagine your freedom, and continue to do so until it is subjectified; then after gestation in the darkness the manifestation comes—your prayer is answered.

Consider for a moment a distinguished, talented architect; he can build a beautiful, modern, twentieth century city in his mind, complete with super highways, swimming pools, aquariums, parks, etc. He can construct in his mind the most beautiful palace that eye has ever seen. He can see the building in its entirety completely erected before he ever gives his plan to the builders. Where was the building? It was in his imagination.

With your imagination you can actually hear the invisible voice of your mother even though she lives 10,000 miles from here. You can also see her clearly, and as vividly as if she were present; this is the wonderful power you possess. *You* can develop and cultivate this power, and become successful and prosperous.

Haven't you heard the sales manager say, "I have to let John go, because his attitude is wrong?"

The business world knows the importance of "right attitude."

I remember many years ago having printed a small article on Reincarnation. These pamphlets were on display on a book counter of a church where I lectured. In the beginning very few of them were sold, because the salesgirl was violently opposed to its contents.

I explained to her the Biblical meaning of Reincarnation, the origin of the story, and what it was all about. She understood the contents of the drama, and became enthusiastic about the booklets; they were all sold before my lecture series was completed. This was an instance of the importance of the right, mental attitude.

Your mental attitude means your mental reaction to people, circumstances, conditions, and objects in space. What is your relationship with your co-workers? Are you friendly with people, with animals, and with the universe in general? Do you think the universe is hostile, and that the world owes you a living? In short what is your *attitude?*

The emotional reaction of the above mentioned girl was one of deep-seated prejudice. That was the *wrong attitude* in selling books; she was biased toward the book and the writer.

You can develop the right, mental attitude when you realize that nothing externally can upset you or hurt you without your mental consent. You are the only thinker in your world; consequently nothing can move you to anger, grief, or sorrow without your mental consent. The suggestions that come to you from the outside have no power whatsoever, except you permit them to move you in thought negatively. Realize you are master of your thought-world. Emotions follow thought; hence you are supreme in your own orbit. Do you permit others to influence you? Do you allow the headlines in the newspapers, or the gossip, or criticism of others to upset you, or bring about mental depression? If you do, you must admit you are the cause of your own mood; you created your emotional reaction. Your attitude is wrong.

Do you imagine evil of others? If you do, notice the emotion generated in your deeper self; it is negative and destructive to your health and prosperity. Circumstances can affect you only as you permit them. You can voluntarily and definitely change your attitude toward life and all things. You can become master of your fate, and

15

captain of your soul (subconscious mind). Through disciplined, directed, and controlled imagination you can dominate and master your emotions and mental attitude in general.

If you imagine, for example, that the other is mean, dishonest, and jealous, notice the emotion you evoked within yourself. Now reverse the situation. Begin to imagine the same girl or boy is honest, sincere, loving, and kind; notice the reaction it calls forth in you. Are you not, therefore, master of your attitudes? In reality the truth of the whole matter is that it is your real concept of God which determines your whole attitude toward life in general. Your dominant idea about God is your idea of life; for God is Life. If you have the dominant idea or attitude that God is the Spiritual Power within you responsive to your thought, and that, therefore, since your habitual thinking is constructive and harmonious, this Power is guiding and prospering you in all ways; this dominant attitude will color everything. You will be looking at the world through the positive, affirmative attitude of mind. Your outlook will be positive, and you will have a joyous expectancy of the best.

Many people have a gloomy, despondent out-

16

look on life. They are sour, cynical, and cantankerous; this is due to the dominant, mental attitude which directs their reaction to everything.

A person's mood of joy is usually short-lived who is constantly singing the blues when something wonderful comes into his experience or that of his family.

A young boy of sixteen years going to high school said to me, "I am getting very poor grades. My memory is failing. I do not know what is the matter." The only thing wrong was his attitude. He adopted a new, mental attitude by realizing how important his studies were in gaining entrance grades to college in order to become a lawyer. He began to pray scientifically, which is one of the quickest ways to change the mentality.

In scientific prayer we deal with a principle which responds to thought. This young man realized there was a Spiritual Power within him, and that It was the only Cause and Power. Furthermore he began to claim that his memory was perfect, and that Infinite Intelligence constantly revealed to him everything he needed to know at all times everywhere. He began to radiate Love and goodwill to the teachers and fellow students. This young man is now enjoying a greater free-

17

dom than he had known for several years. He constantly imagines the teachers and his mother congratulating him on all "A's." It is imagining the desired results that have followed this change of attitude toward his studies.

We have said previously that all our mental attitudes are conditioned by imagination. If you imagine: It is going to be a black day today; business is going to be very poor; that it is raining; no customers will come into your store; they have no money, etc., you will experience the result of your negative imagery.

One time Troward was walking the streets of London, and he imagined he saw a snake on the street. Fear caused him to become semi-paralyzed. What he saw *looked* like a snake, but Troward had the same mental and emotional reaction as if it were a snake.

Imagine whatsoever things are lovely, noble, and of good report, and your entire emotional attitude toward life will change. What do you imagine about life? Is it going to be a happy life for you? Or is it one long series of frustrations? "Choose ye whom ye will serve."

You mold, fashion, and shape your outer world of experience according to the mental images you habitually dwell on. Imagine conditions and circumstances in life which dignify, elevate, please, and satisfy. If you imagine life is cold, cruel, hard, bitter, and that struggle and pain are inevitable, you are making life miserable for yourself.

Imagine yourself on the golf course. You are free, relaxed, full of enthusiasm, and energy. Your joy is in overcoming all the difficulties presented by the golf course. The thrill is in surmounting all the obstacles.

Now let us take this scene: Imagine yourself going into a funeral parlor. Notice the different, emotional response brought forward as you picture yourself in each of the above mentioned situations. In the funeral chapel you can rejoice in the person's new birthday. You can imagine the loved one surrounded by his or her friends in the midst of indescribable beauty and love. You can imagine God's river of peace flooding the minds and hearts of all present. You can actually ascend the heavens of your own mind wherever you are; this is the Power of your imagination.

"And he dreamed yet another dream, and told it his brethren, and said, Behold, I have dreamed a dream more; and behold, the sun and the moon and the eleven stars made obeisance to me."

19

BELIEVE IN YOURSELF

In ancient symbology, the *sun and the moon* represent the conscious and subconscious mind. The eleven stars represent the eleven powers in addition to imagination. Here again the inspired writers are telling you that disciplined imagination takes precedence over all other faculties of the mind, and controls the direction of the conscious and subconscious mind. Imagination is first and foremost; it can be scientifically directed.

I was examining one of the Round Towers of Ireland with my father over fifty years ago. He said nothing for one hour, but remained passive and receptive, seeming to be in a pensive mood. I asked him what was he meditating on? This is the essence of his answer: He pointed out that it is only by dwelling on the great, wonderful ideas of the world that we grow and expand. He contemplated the age of the stones in the tower; then his imagination took him back to the quarries where stones were first formed. His imagination unclothed the stones. He saw with the interior eye the structure, the geological formation, the composition of the stone, and reduced it to the formless state; finally he imagined the oneness of the stones with all stones and with all life. He realized in his Divine imagery that it was possible to re-

construct the history of the Irish race from looking at the Round Tower!

Through the imaginative faculty this teacher
was able to see the invisible men living in the
Tower and to hear their voices. The whole place
became alive to him in his imagination. Through
this power he was able to go back in time when
there was no Round Tower there. In his mind
he began to weave a drama of the place from
which stones originated, who brought them, the
purpose of the structure, and the history connected
with it. As he said to me, "I am able to almost
feel the touch, and hear the sound of steps that
vanished thousands of years ago."

The subjective mind permeates all things; it is in
all things, and is the substance from which they
are made. The treasure-house of eternity is in
the very stones comprising a building. There is
nothing inanimate; all is life in its varied mani-
festions. (The sun and the moon make obeisance
to Joseph —imagination.) Truly through your faculty of imagination you can imagine the invisible
secrets of nature are revealed to you; you will find
that you can plumb the very depths of consciousness calling things that be not as though they were,
and the unseen becomes seen.

21

BELIEVE IN YOURSELF

The other night I sat in a park, and looked at the setting sun. Suddenly I began to think that the sun is like a house in the City of Los Angeles; there is a greater sun behind our sun, and so on to Infinity. It staggers the imagination to ponder and meditate on the myriads of suns and solar galaxies extending into infinity beyond the milky way. This world is only a grain of sand in the infinite seashore. Instead of seeing the parts, let us look at the wholeness, the unity of all things. We are, as the poet said, "All parts of one stupendous whole, whose body nature is, and God the soul."

It is really out of the imaginative mind of man all religions are born. Is it not out of the realm of imagination television, radio, radar, superjets, and all other modern inventions came? Your imagination is the treasure-house of Infinity, which releases to you all the precious jewels of music, art, poetry, and inventions. You can look at some ancient ruin, an old temple, or pyramid, and reconstruct the records of the dead past. In the ruins of an old church yard you can also see a modern city resurrected in all its beauty and glory. You may be in a prison of want, lack, or behind stone bars, but in your imagination you can find an undreamed of measure of freedom.

Remember how Chico, the Parisian sewer cleaner, imagined and lived in a paradisaical state of mind called the seventh heaven even though he never saw the light of day.

Bunyan in prison wrote the great masterpiece, *Pilgrim's Progress*. Milton though blind saw with the interior eye. His imagination made his brain a ball of fire, and he wrote *Paradise Lost*. In this way he brought some of God's Paradise to all men everywhere.

Imagination was Milton's spiritual eye which enabled him to go about God's business whereby he annihilated time, space, and matter, and brought forth the truths of the Invisible Presence and Power.

A genius is a man who is en-rapport with his subconscious mind. He is able to tap this universal reservoir, and receive answers to his problems; thus he does not have to work by the sweat of his brow. In the genius type of mind the imaginative faculty is developed to a very high degree. All great poets and writers are gifted with a highly developed and cultivated imaginative faculty.

I can now see Shakespeare listening to the old stories, fables, and myths of his day. I can also imagine him sitting down listing all these characters in the play in his mind; then clothing them one by one with hair, skin, muscle, bone, animating them, and making them so much alive that we think we are reading about ourselves.

Use your imagination, and go about your Father's business. *Your Father's business* is to let your wisdom, skill, knowledge, and ability come forth, and bless others as well as yourself. You are about your Father's business if you are operating a small store, and in your imagination you feel you are operating a larger store giving a greater measure of service to your fellow creature.

If you are a writer of short stories, you can be about your Father's business. Create a story in your mind which teaches something about the Golden rule; then pass that story and all its characters through your spiritualized and highly artistic mentality; your article will be fascinating and intensely interesting to your public.

The truth about man is always wonderful and beautiful. When writing a novel or story, we should be sure that we clothe Truth in her garment of Loveliness and Beauty. You could now

24

look at an acorn, and with your imaginative eye construct a magnificent forest full of rivers, rivulets, and streams. You could people the forest with all kinds of life; furthermore you could hang a bow on every cloud. You could look at a desert, and cause it to rejoice and blossom as a rose. "Instead of the thorn shall come up the fir tree, and instead of the brier shall come up the myrtle tree." Men gifted with intuition and imagination find water in the desert, and they create cities where formerly other men only saw a desert and a wilderness.

An architect of a city sees the buildings and fountains already in operation before he ever digs a well or builds a house. "I will make the wilderness a pool of water, and the dry land springs of water."

Long hours, hard labor, or burning the midnight oil will not produce a Milton, a Shakespeare, a Phidias, or a Beethoven. Men accomplish great things through quiet moments imagining that the invisible things of Him from the foundation of time are clearly visible.

You can imagine the Indescribable Beauty of He Who Is is being expressed on your canvas, and if you are a real artist in love with beauty, great beauty will come forth effortlessly. Moments of great inspiration will come to you; it will have nothing to do with perspiration or hard, mental labor.

In Greenwich Village I met a poet who wrote beautiful poems; he had them printed on cards, and sold them at Christmas time. Some of these poems were beautiful gems of spiritual love. He said when he got still, the words would come into his mind accompanied by a lovely scene. Flowers, people, and friends would come clearly into his mind. These images spoke to him. They told him their story. Oftentimes the complete poem, song, or lullaby would appear complete and ready in his mind without the slightest effort. His habit was to imagine he was writing beautiful poems which would stir the hearts of men.

Shelley said poetry was an expression of the imagination. When the poet meditates on Love, and wishes to write on Love, the Invisible Intelligence and Wisdom within him stirs his mind, casts the spell of God's beauty over him, and awakens him to God's Eternal Love, so that his words become clothed with wisdom, truth, and beauty.

The Great Musician is within. If it is your business to play music or compose music, be sure you are on your Father's Business. Your *Father's Business* is first of all to recognize God as the Great Musician; then meditate, feel, pray, and know that the Inner Music sings or plays through you the Song of God's Love, and you will play like you never played before.

Every invention of Edison's was first conceived in his imagination. The same was true of Tesla, another great inventor and scientist.

I think it was Oliver Wendall Holmes who said we need three story men who can idealize, imagine, and predict. I believe it was the capacity to imagine and dream that caused Ford to look forward to putting the world on wheels.

Your capacity to imagine causes you, and enables you to remove all barriers of time and space. You can reconstruct the past or contemplate the future thought through your inner eye. No wonder it says in Genesis, "Israel loved Joseph [imagination] more than all his brethren." Imagination when disciplined, spiritualized, controlled, and directed becomes the most exalted and noblest attribute of man.

I was in conversation some years ago with a

young chemist, who stated that his superiors for
years had tried to manufacture a certain German
dye and failed. He was given the assignment when
he went with them. As he commented, he did not
know it could not be done, and synthesized the
compound without any difficulty. They were
amazed and wanted to know his secret. His answer was that he imagined he had the answer.
Pressed further by his superiors he said that he
could clearly see the letters, "Answer!" in blaz-
ing red color in his mind; then he created a vacu-
um underneath the letters knowing that as he
imagined the chemical formula underneath the
letters, the subconscious would fill it in. The third
night he had a dream, in which the complete
formula and the technique of making the compound was clearly presented.

"Joseph [imagination] is a dreamer, and a
dreamer of dreams." "They conspired against him
to slay him. And they said one to another, Behold,
this dreamer cometh." Perhaps as you read these
Biblical quotations there are thoughts of fear,
doubt, and anxiety conspiring in your own mind
to slay or kill that desire, ideal, or dream of yours.
You look at conditions or circumstances, and fear
arises in your mind; yet there is the desire with-

in you which if realized would bring you peace and solve your problem.

You must be like Joseph, and become a practical dreamer. Decide to make your dreams come true. Withdraw and abstract your attention now from appearances of things and from sense evidence. Even though your senses deny what you pray for, affirm it as true in your heart. Bring your mind back from its wandering after the false Gods of fear and doubt to rest in the Omnipotence of the Spiritual Power within you. In the silence and quietude of your own mind, dwell on the fact that there is only One Power and One Presence. This Power and Presence is now responding to your thought as guidance, strength, peace, and nourishment for the soul. Give all your mental attention to recognizing the absolute sovereignty of the Spiritual Power knowing that the God-Power has the answer, and is now showing you the way. Trust It; believe in It, and walk the earth in the Light your prayer is already answered.

All of us read the story of Columbus and his discovery of America. It was imagination that led him to his discovery. His imagination plus faith in a Divine Power led him on, and brought him to victory.

The sailors said to Columbus, "What shall we do when all hope is gone?"

His reply was, "You shall say at break of day, 'Sail on, sail on, and on.' " Here is the key to prayer; be faithful to the end; full of faith every step of the way, persisting to the end, knowing in your heart the end is secure, because you saw the end. Having seen and felt the end, as Troward said, you have willed the means to the realization of the end.

Copernicus through his vivid imagination revealed how the earth revolved on its axis, causing the old astronomical theories to be cast in the discard.

I think it would be a wonderful idea if all of us from time to time recast our ideas, checked up on our beliefs and opinions, and asked ourselves honestly, "Why do I believe that? Where did that opinion come from?" Perhaps many ideas, theories, beliefs, and opinions which we hold are completely erroneous, and were accepted by us as true without any investigation whatever as to their truth or accuracy. Because our father and grand-

30

father believed in a certain way is no reason why we should.

One woman said to me that a certain idea she had must be true, because her grandmother believed it. That is absurd! The race mind believes in many things which are not true. What came down from generation to generation is not necessarily valid or the final word and authority.

The above mentioned woman who was honest and well-meaning had a mind that was very touchy on psychological truths. She took everything in the Bible literally. This mind worked by prejudice, superstition, and opposed everything which was not in accord with her established beliefs, opinions, and preconceived notions.

Our mind must be like a parachute. The latter opens up; if it does not, it isn't any good. Likewise we must open our eyes and minds to new truths. We must hunger and thirst after new truth and new knowledge, enabling us to soar aloft above our problems on the wings of faith and understanding.

The famous biologists, physicists, astronomers, and mathematicians of our day are men gifted with a vivid, scientific imagination. For instance

31

the Einstein theory of relativity existed first in his imaginaton.

Archaeologists and paleontologists studying the tombs of ancient Egypt through their imaginative perception reconstruct ancient scenes. The dead past becomes alive and audible once more. Looking at the ancient ruins and the hieroglyphics thereon, the scientist tells us of an age when there was no language. Communication was done by grunts, groans, and signs. The scientist's imagination enables him to clothe this ancient temple with roofs, and surround them with gardens, pools, and fountains. The fossil remains are clothed with eyes, sinews, and muscles, and they again walk and talk. The past becomes the living present, and we find in imagination there is no time or space. Through your imaginative faculty you can be a companion of the most inspired writers of all time.

I gave a lecture on the twenty first chapter of Revelation some time ago in the Wilshire Ebell Theatre in Los Angeles to our Sunday audience. The previous night while I was meditating on the inner meaning of the following verses, I intuitively and actually felt the presence and the

32

intimate companionship of the mystic seer who
wrote the inspired verses.

"And I John saw the holy city, new Jerusalem,
coming down from God out of heaven, prepared
as a bride adorned for her husband. And I heard
a great voice out of heaven saying, Behold, the
tabernacle of God is with men, and he will dwell
with them, and be their God." (Rev. 21:2, 2)

Can't you now walk down the corridor of your
own mind, and there see, inwardly perceive, feel,
and sense God's river of peace flowing through
your mind? You are now in the Holy City—your
own mind—inhabited by such lovely people as
bliss, joy, faith, harmony, love, and good will.
Your mind is clothed with God's radiant beauty,
and your mood is exalted, noble, and God-like.
You are married mentally and spiritually to God
and to all things good. You have on your wedding
garment, because you are in tune with the Infinite, and God's Eternal Verities constantly impregnate your mind. In your imagination you
sense and feel that you are the tabernacle of God,
and that His Holy Spirit saturates and fills every
part of your being. Your imagination now becomes
seized with a Divine frenzy. You become God-
intoxicated, having received the Divine antibody,

the Presence of God in the chamber of your heart.

You can look at a rock, and out of that rock through Divine Imagination you can reveal the Madonna, and portray a vision of beauty and a joy forever. Never permit your imagination to be used negatively; never distort or twist it. You can imagine sickness, accident, and loss, and become a mental wreck. To imagine sickness and lack is to destroy your peace of mind, health, and happiness.

On board ship one time I heard a passenger exclaim when looking at the setting sun, "I am so happy, I hope this lasts forever!"

How often have you seen a glorious sunrise—perhaps you said, "I hope this lasts forever?" Nothing in this transitory world lasts eternally; however the Truths of God last forever. Darkness follows night, but morning will come again. Twilight will also come. You do not want things to stand still. You do not want to stand still either; for there are new worlds within and without to conquer. Change eternal is at the root of all life.

You do not want to remain in a rut. Problems are life's way of asking you for an answer. The greatest joy and satisfaction is in overcoming, in

34

conquering. Life would become unbearable and unendurable if we did not experience change. We would be bored by the monotony of things. You meet with night and day, cold and heat, ebb and flow, summer and winter, hope and despair, success and failure. You find yourself moving through opposites; through your power to imagine what you wish and to feel its reality subjectively is to reconcile the opposites, and bring peace to the mind.

In the midst of sorrow, grief, or the loss of a loved one, your imagination and faith, the two wings of the bird, take you aloft into the very Bosom of God, your Father, where you find peace, solace, and Divine rest for your soul.

In your imagination you look into the very Face or Truth of God, and God wipes away all tears, and there shall be no more crying. All the mist and fog of the human mind dissolves in the sunshine of God's Love.

"And God shall wipe away all tears from their eyes; and there shall be no more death, neither sorrow, nor crying; neither, shall there be any more pain: for the former things are passed away. Behold I make all things new." (Rev. 4, 5.)

When the night is black, you see no way out; i.e., when your problem is most acute, let your imagination be your saviour.

"I will lift up mine eyes [imagination] unto the hills, from whence cometh my help." (Ps. 121:1.) *The hills* are of an inner range—the Presence of God in you. When you seek guidance and inspiration, fix your eyes on the stars of God's Truth, such as "Infinite Intelligence leads and guides me," or "Divine Wisdom floods my mind, and I am inspired from on High."

There is a designer, an architect, and a weaver within you; it takes the fabric of your mind, your thoughts, feelings, and beliefs, and moulds them into a pattern of life which brings you peace or discord, health or sickness. You can imagine a life which will take you up to the third heaven where you will see unspeakable and unutterable things of God, or through the distorted, morbid use of your imagination you can sink to the depths of degradation.

Man is the tabernacle of God, and no matter how low a man has sunk, the Healing Presence is there waiting to minister to him. It is within us waiting for us to call upon It. You can use

36

your imagination in all business transactions in a wonderful way. Always imagine yourself in the other fellow's place; this tells you what to do. Imagine the other is expressing all that you long to see him express. See him as he ought to be, not as he appears to be. Perhaps he is surly, sarcastic, bitter, hostile; there may be many frustrated hopes and tragedies lurking in his mind. Imagine whatsoever things are lovely and of good report, and through your imagination you have covered him with the garment of God. God's world of ideals and God's infinite ideas are within him waiting to be born and released. You can say if you wish, "God waits to be born in him." You can open the door, and kindle the fire of God's Love in that man's heart, and perhaps the spark you lit will burst into a Divine Fire.

The greatest and richest galleries of art in the world are the galleries of the mind devoted to God's Truths and Beauty. Leonardo Da Vinci through his gift of imagination meditated on Jesus and the Twelve Disciples, and what they meant. Lost in deep revery, his imagination secreted the perfect pictures from the Infinite Reservoir within him, and due to his perfect focus his inner eye glowed with an interior luminosity, so that he was inspired, and out of his Divine Imagery came the masterpiece—The Last Supper.

You have visited a quiet lake or a mountain top. Notice how the placid, cool, calm surface reflected the heavenly lights, so does the quiet mind of the spiritual man reflect God's interior Lights and Wisdom.

Picture your ideal in life; live with this ideal. Let the ideal captivate your imagination; let the ideal thrill you! You will move in the direction of the ideal which governs your mind. The ideals of life are like the dew of heaven which move over the arid areas of man's mind refreshing and invigorating him.

The inspired writer's imagination was fired with Truth when he wrote, "There is a river the streams whereof shall make glad the city of God, the holy place of the tabernacles of the most High." (Ps. 46:4.)

By now you know that imagination is the river enabling *you* to flow back psychologically to God. The streams and rivulets are your ideas and feelings, plus the emanation of love and good will that goes forth from you to all men everywhere.

Man looks out into the world, and he sees

sickness, chaos, and man's inhumanity to man. The man with the disciplined imagination soars above all appearances, discord, sense evidence, and sees the sublime principle of harmony operating through, in, and behind all things. He knows through his Divine imagery that there is an Everlasting Law of Righteousness behind all things, an Ever Abiding Peace, a Boundless Love governing the entire Cosmos. These Truths surge through the heart, and are born of the eternal Truth which through the imagination pierces the outer veil, and rests in the Divine meaning of the way it is in God and Heaven.

Imagination was the workshop of God which inspired the writer of the following matchless, spiritual gems which will go down through the corridor of time, and live forever. For tender beauty and for Divine imagery they are unsurpassed in dealing with the availability and Immanence of God's Presence.

"For he shall give his angels charge over thee, to keep thee in all thy ways." (Ps. 91:11.)

"Whither shall I go from thy spirit? or whither shall I flee from thy presence?

"If I ascend up into heaven, thou art there: if I make my bed in hell, behold, thou *art there.*

"If I take the wings of the morning, and dwell in the uttermost parts of the sea;

"Even there shall thy hand lead me, and thy right hand shall hold me."

USING THE SUBCONSCIOUS MIND
IN BUSINESS

Long before our Bible was published ancient wisdom said, "As a man imagines and feels, so does he become." This ancient teaching is lost in the night of time; it is lost in antiquity.

The Bible states, "As a man thinketh in his heart so is he."

Legend relates that many thousands of years ago the Chinese sages gathered together under the leadership of a great sage, to discuss the fact that vast legends of brutal invaders were pillaging and plundering the land. The question to be resolved was, "How shall we preserve the ancient wisdom from the destruction of the invaders?"

There were many suggestions: Some thought that the ancient scrolls and symbols should be buried in the Himalayan Mountains. Others suggested that the wisdom be deposited in monasteries in Tibet. Still others pointed out that the sacred temples of India were the ideal places for the preservation of the wisdom of their God.

The chief sage was silent during the entire discussion; in fact he went to sleep in the midst of their talk, and snored loudly, much to their dismay! He awakened in a little while, and said, "Tao [God] gave me the answer, and it is this: 'We will order the great pictorial artists of China, —men gifted with Divine imagination,—[which is the workshop of God] and tell them what we wish to accomplish. We will initiate them into the mysteries of Truth. They will portray or depict in picture form, the great Truths which shall be preserved for all time, and for countless generations yet unborn. When they are finished with the dramatization of the great Truths, Powers, Qualities, and Attributes of God through a series of picture cards, we will tell the world about a new game that has been originated. Men throughout the world for all time will use them as a game of chance, not knowing that through this simple device, they are preserving the sacred teaching for all generations.' " This was the origin of our own deck of cards.

The ancient Chinese sage according to the legend added, "If all the sacred writings were destroyed, they could again be resurrected at any time through the symbolic teachings and inner meanings of the various designs on the playing cards."

Imagination clothes all ideas, and gives them form. These artists through the Divine artistry of imagination clothed all these ideas with pictorial form. In the act of imagination that which is hidden in your deeper self is made manifest. By imagination what exists in latency or is asleep within you is given form in thought. We contemplate that which hitherto had been unrevealed.

Let us take some simple examples: When you were going to be married, you had vivid, realistic pictures in your mind. With your power of imagination you saw the minister or priest. You heard him pronounce the words; you saw the flowers, the church, and you heard the music. You imagined the ring on your finger, and you travelled through your imagination on your honeymoon to Niagara or Europe. All this was performed by your imagination.

Likewise before graduation, you had a beautiful, scenic drama taking place in your mind; you had clothed all your ideas about graduation in form. You imagined the professor or the president of the college giving you your diploma. You saw all the students dressed in gowns. You heard your mother, or father, or your girl friend congratulate you. You felt the embrace and the kiss; it was all real, dramatic, exciting, and wonderful. Images appeared freely in your mind as if from nowhere, but you know and must admit there was and is an Internal Creator with Power to mould all these forms which you saw in your mind, and endow them with life, motion, and voice. These images said to you, "For you only we live!"

A young man said to me in the army before he was discharged, "I see my mother clearly. I can now imagine her welcome. I see the old home. Father is smoking a pipe. My sister is feeding the dogs. I can see every mark and corner of that home. I can even hear their voices."

Where do all these vivid pictures come from? Keats said that there is an ancestral wisdom in man, and we can, if we wish, drink of that old wine of heaven.

The spirit or God in you is the real basis of imagination. Once in an examination in London, I did not know the answer to an important question. I got still and quiet, and said over and over again slowly, meditating in a relaxed way, "God reveals the answer!" In the meantime I went on answering the other questions which were easy.

We know that when you relax the conscious mind, the subjective wisdom rises to the fore. In a short while the picture of the answer came clearly into my mind. It was there in words like a page of a book with the entire answer written out as a graph in the mind. A Mightier Wisdom than that of my conscious mind or intellect spoke through me.

I had a very religious school boy about 14 years old come to me. Whenever he had a problem, he said to me that he would imagine Jesus was talking to him giving him the answer to his problem, and telling him what to do. His mother was very ill; this boy was highly imaginative. He read the story of Jesus healing the woman with fever. My little friend related to me, "Last night I imagined Jesus saying to me, "Go thy way; thy mother is made whole!" He made that drama of the mind so real, vivid, and intense, that due to his faith and belief he convinced himself of the truth of what he heard subjectively.

His mother was completely healed; yet she was considered at that time hopeless and beyond medical help.

45

Being a student of the laws of mind, you know what happened. He galvanized himself into the feeling of being one with his image, and according to his faith or conviction was it done unto him. There is only One Mind and One Healing Presence. As the boy changed his conviction about his mother, and felt her perfect health, the idea of perfect health was resurrected in her mind simultaneously. He did not know anything about spiritual healing or the power of imagination. He operated the law unconsciously, and believed in his own mind that Jesus was actually talking to him; then according to his belief was it done unto him.

To believe something is to accept it as true. This is why Paracelsus said in the 16th century, "Whether the object of your belief be true or false, you will get the same results." There is only one spiritual, healing Principle and one Process of healing called *faith*. "According to your faith is it done unto you." There are many processes, methods, and techniques of healing, and all of them get results—not because of the particular technique or method, but because of imagination and faith in the particular process. They are all tapping the One Source of healing which is God. The

46

Infinite Healing Presence permeates all things and is Omnipresent.

The voodoo doctor with his incantations gets results. So does the Kahuna of Hawaii with his ministrations, the various branches of New Thought, Christian Science, the Nancy School of Medicine, Osteopathy, etc. get healings. All these schools of thought are meeting levels of consciousness, and are doing good.

Any method or process which alleviates human misery, pain, and distress is good. Many churches practice laying on of hands; others make novenas and visit shrines; all are benefited according to their mental acceptance or belief.

When you are willing to stand alone with God, and cease completely giving power to external things; when you no longer give power to the phenomenalistic world, which means to make a world of effect a cause; when all your allegiance is given to the Spiritual Power within you, realizing it as the only Presence and the only Cause, you will not need any props of any kind. The Living Intelligence which made your body will respond immediately to your faith and understanding, and you will have an instantaneous, spiritual healing. If you are not at that level of consciousness where you can grow a tooth through prayer, the obvious thing to do is to go see a dentist; pray for him and for a perfect, Divine, oral adjustment. As long as you believe in external causes, you will seek external remedies.

To illustrate further the power of imagination, I will tell you of a close relative of mine who had tuberculosis. His lungs were badly diseased. His son decided to heal his father. He came home to Perth, Western Australia, where his father lived, and said to him that he had met a monk who sold him a piece of the true cross, and that he gave him the equivalent of $500 for it. (This young man had picked up a splinter of wood off the sidewalk, went to a jeweler's and had it set in a ring so that it looked real.) He told his father that many were healed just by touching the ring or the cross. He inflamed and fired his father's imagination to the point that the old gentleman snatched the ring from him, placed it over his chest, prayed silently, and went to sleep. In the morning he was healed; all the clinic's tests were negative.

You know, of course, it was not the splinter of wood from the sidewalk that healed him. It was his imagination aroused to an intense degree, plus the confident expectancy of a perfect healing. Imagination was joined to faith or subjective feeling, and the union of the two brought about the healing. The father never learned the trick that had been played upon him; if he had, he probably would have had a relapse. He remained completely cured, and passed away 15 years later at the age of 89.

I know a business man here in Los Angeles who has reached the top in his field. He told me that for 30 years the most important decisions he ever made were based on his imaginary conversations with Paul. I asked him to elaborate, and he remarked that few people in the business world realized the wonderful guidance and counsel they could receive by dramatizing in their imagination that they were receiving counsel from the writers or great seers of the Bible.

I will quote this successful executive as accurately as I can. "Many times my decisions might have prospered the company or plunged it into bankruptcy. I vacillated, wavered, got high blood pressure, and heart disease. One day the idea came to me why not ask Jesus or Paul. I loved the Epistles of Paul, so when an important decision was to be made, I would imagine Paul was saying to me: 'Your decision is perfect; it will bless your organization. Bless you, my son! Keep on God's path.' After imagining I saw Paul and heard him, a wave of peace and inner tranquillity would seize me; I was at peace about all decisions."

This was this business man's way of receiving Divine Guidance by using his imagination to convince himself that right action was his. There is only one Principle of Intelligence in this world; all that is really necessary is to say and believe, "God is guiding me now, and there is only right action in my life."

The mind, as Troward tells you, works like a syllogism. If your premise is correct, the conclusion or result will correspond. The subjective reasons deductively only, and its sequence or conclusion is always in harmony with the premise. Establish the right premise in your mind; you will be subjectively compelled to right action. Inner movement of the mind is action. The external movements and action is the automatic response of the body to the internal motion of the mind. Hearing a friend or associate congratulate you on your wonderful decision will induce the movement of right action in your life.

50

The man who used St. Paul to impregnate his mind with the belief of right action was using the One Eternal Principle of Intelligence. His technique of arriving at that place in his mind does not really matter.

Goethe used his imagination wisely when confronted with difficulties and predicaments. His biographers point out that he was accustomed to fill many hours quietly holding imaginary conversations. It is well-known that his custom was to imagine one of his friends before him in a chair answering in the right way. In other words if he were concerned over any problems, he imagined his friend was giving him the right or appropriate answer, accompanied with the usual gestures, tonal qualities of the voice, making the entire imaginery scene as real and vivid as possible.

I was very well acquainted with a stock broker in New York City, who used to attend my classes at Steinway Hall there. His method of solving financial difficulties was very simple. He would have mental, imaginary conversations with a multimillionaire banker-friend of his who used to congratulate him on his wise and sound judgment, and compliment him on his purchase of the right stocks. He used to dramatize this imaginary conversation until he had psychologically fixed it as a form of belief in his mind.

Mr. Nicols, Ouspensky's student, used to say, "Watch your inner talking, and let it agree with your aim."

This broker's inner talking or speech certainly agreed with his aim to make sound investments for himself and his clients. He told me his main purpose in his business life was to make money for others, and to see them prosper financially by his wise counsel. It is quite obvious he was using the laws of mind constructively.

Prayer is a habit. This broker regularly and at frequent intervals during the day returned to the mental image in his mind; he made it a deep, subjective pattern. That which is embodied subjectively is objectively expressed. It is the *sustained* mental picture which is developed in the dark house of the mind. Run your mental movie often. Get into the habit of flashing it on the screen of your mind frequently. After awhile it will become a definite, habitual pattern. The inner movie which you have seen with your mind's eye shall be made manifest openly, "He calleth things that be not as though they were, and the unseen becomes seen."

Many people solve their dilemmas and problems by the play of their imagination, knowing that whatever they imagine and feel as true will and must come to pass.

Sometime ago, a certain young woman was involved in a complicated law suit which had persisted for five years. There was one postponement after another with no solution in sight. At my suggestion she began to dramatize as vividly as possible her lawyer having an animated discussion with her regarding the outcome. She would ask him questions, and he would answer her appropriately; then she condensed the whole thing down to a simple phrase as suggested years ago by the French School of Mental Therapeutics. She had him repeat it over and over again to her. The phrase she said was, "There has been a perfect, harmonious solution. The whole case is settled outside court." She kept looking at the mental picture whenever she had a spare moment. While in a restaurant for a cup of coffee, she ran the mental movie with gestures, voice, and sound equipment. She could imagine easily the sound of his voice, smile, and mannerism. She ran the movie so often, it became a subjective pattern—a regular train track. It was written in her mind;

or as the Bible says, it was "written in her heart and inscribed in her inward parts." Her conclusion was, "It is God in action," meaning all round harmony and peace. (*Harmony* is of God, and what you want in a legal case is a harmonious solution.)

In the science of imagination you must first of all begin to discipline your imagination, and not let it run riot. *Science* insists upon purity. If you wish a chemically pure product, you must remove all traces of other substances as well as extraneous material. You must in other words separate out and cast away all the dross.

In the science of imagination you eliminate all the mental impurities, such as fear, worry, destructive inner talking, self condemnation, and the mental union with other miscellaneous negatives. You must focus all your attention on your ideal, and refuse to be swerved from your purpose or aim in life. As you get mentally absorbed in the reality of your ideal, by loving and remaining faithful to it, you will see your desire take form in your world. In the book of Joshua it says, "Choose ye this day whom ye shall serve." Let your choice be, "I am going to imagine whatsoever things are lovely and of good report."

I know and have talked to many people who

diabolically invert the use of their God-given faculty. The mother, e.g., imagines something bad has happened to her son, John, because he is late coming home. She imagines an accident, a hospital, Johnny in the operating room, etc.

A business man whose affairs are prospering, yet dwells on negativity, is another example of the destructive use of imagination. He comes home from the office, runs a motion picture in his mind of failure, sees the shelves empty, imagines himself going into bankruptcy, an empty bank balance, and the business closed down; yet all the time he is actually prospering. There is no truth whatsoever in that negative, mental picture of his; it is a lie made out of whole cloth. In other words the thing he fears does not exist save in his morbid imagination; the failure will never come to pass, except he keeps up that morbid picture charged with the emotion of fear. If he constantly indulges in this mental picture, he will, of course, bring failure to pass. He had the choice of failure or success, but he chose failure.

There are chronic worriers; they never seem to imagine anything good or lovely. They seem to know that always something bad or destructive is going to happen. They cannot tell you one reason why something good should and could happen; however they are ready with all the reasons why something dire and evil should occur.

Why is this? The reason is simple; these people are habitually negative; i.e., most of their thinking is of a negative, chaotic, destructive, morbid nature. As they continue to make a habit of these negative patterns of thought, they condition their subconscious mind negatively. Their imagination is governed by their dominant moods and feelings; this is why they imagine evil even about their loved ones.

For example, if their son happens to be in the army, they imagine he is going to catch cold, become an alcoholic, become loose morally; or if he is in combat they imagine he will be shot, and all manner of destructive images enter their mind. This is due to the hypnotic spell of habit, and their prayers are rendered null and void.

Make a choice now! Begin to think constructively and harmoniously. *To think* is to speak. Your thought is your word. Let your words be as a honeycomb, sweet to the ear, and pleasant to the bones." Let your words be "like apples of Gold in pictures of silver." The future is the present grown up; it is your invisible word or thought made visible. Are your words sweet to the ear? What is your inner speech like at this moment? No one heard you; it is your own silent thought. Perhaps you are saying to yourself, "I can't; it is impossible." "I'm too old now." "What chance have I?" "Mary can, but I can't. I have no money. I can't afford this or that. I've tried; it's no use." You can see your words are not as a honeycomb; they are not sweet to your ear; they do not lift you up or inspire you.

Ouspensky was always stressing the importance of inner speech, inner conversation, or inner talking. It is really the way you feel inside; for the inside mirrors the outside. Is your inner speech pleasant to the bones? Does it exalt you, thrill you, and make you happy?

Bones are symbolic of support and symmetry. Let your inner talking sustain and strengthen you. "But the word is very nigh unto thee, in thy mouth, and in thy heart, that thou mayest do it. See I have set before thee this day life and good, and death and evil."

Decree now, and say it meaningly: "From this moment forward I will admit to my mind for mental consumption only those ideas and thoughts which heal, bless, inspire, and strengthen me."

Let your words from now on be as "apples of gold in pictures of silver." An apple is a delicious fruit. *Gold* means power. *Pictures of silver* mean in the Bible your desires. The *picture* in your mind is the way you want things to be. It is the picture of your fulfilled desire. It could be a new position or health. Let your words, your inner silent thought, and feeling coincide and agree with the *Picture of silver* or your desire. Desire and feeling joined together in a mental marriage will become the answered prayer.

Be sure you follow the imagination of the Bible, and let your words be sweet to the ear. What are you giving *your ear* to now. What are you listening to? What are you giving attention to? Whatever you give attention to will grow, magnify, and multiply in your experience.

"Faith cometh by hearing," Paul says. Listen to the great truths of God. Listen to the voice of God. What language does He speak in? It is not Gaelic, French, Italian, but the universal language or mood of love, peace, joy, harmony, faith, confidence, and goodwill. Give your ear to these qualities and potencies of God. Mentally eat of these qualities and as you continue to do so, you

58

will be conditioned to those positive, enduring qualities, and the Law of Love will govern you.

You have heard this oft repeated quotation, "Man is made in the image and likeness of God." This means your mind is God's mind, as there is only One Mind. Your Spirit is God's Spirit, and you create in exactly the same way, and through the same law as God creates. Your individual world, i.e., experiences, conditions, circumstances, environment, as well as your physical health, financial states, social life, etc., is made out of your own mental images and after your own likeness. Like attracts like. Your world is a mirror reflecting back to you your inner world of thought, feeling, beliefs, and inner conversation. If you begin to imagine evil powers working against you, or that there is a jinx following you, or that other forces and people are working against you, there will be a response of your deeper mind to correspond with these negative pictures and fears in your mind; therefore you will begin to say that everything is against you, or that the stars are opposed to you, or you will blame karma, your past lives, or some demon.

Truly the only sin is ignorance. Pain is not a punishment; it is the consequence of the misuse of your inner power. Come back to the one Truth, and realize that there is only One Spiritual Power, and It functions through the thoughts and images of your mind. The problems, vexations, and strife are due to the fact that man has actually wandered away after false Gods of fear and error. He must return to the center—the God-Presence within. Affirm now the sovereignty and authority of this Spiritual Power within you— the Principle of all life. Claim Divine guidance, strength, nourishment, and peace, and this Power will respond accordingly.

I will now proceed to point out how you may definitely and positively convey an idea or mental image to your subconscious mind. The conscious mind of man is personal and selective. It chooses, selects, weighs, analyzes, dissects, and investigates. It is capable of inductive and deductive reasoning. The subjective or subconscious mind is subject to the conscious mind. It might be called a servant of the conscious mind. The subconscious obeys the order of the conscious mind. Your conscious thought has power. The power you are acquainted with is thought. Back of your thought is Mind, Spirit, or God. Focussed, directed thoughts reach the subjective levels; they must be of a certain degree of intensity. Intensity is acquired by concentration.

To *concentrate* is to come back to the centre and contemplate the Infinite Power within you which lies stretched in smiling repose. To concentrate properly you still the wheels of your mind, and enter into a quiet, relaxed, mental state. When you concentrate, you gather your thoughts together, and you focus all your attention on your ideal, aim, or objective. You are now at a focal or central point, where you are giving all your attention and devotion to your mental image. The procedure of focussed attention is somewhat similar to that of a magnifying glass, and the focus it makes of the rays of the sun. You can see the difference in the effect of scattered vibrations of the sun's heat, and the vibrations which emanate from a central point. You can direct the rays of the magnifying glass, so it will burn up a particular object upon which it is directed. Focussed, steadied attention of your mental images gains a similar intensity, and a deep, lasting impression is made on the sensitive plate of the subconscious mind.

You may have to repeat this drama of the mind many times before an impression is made, but the secret of impregnating the deeper mind is continuous or sustained imagination. When fear or worry comes to you during the day, you can always immediately gaze upon that lovely picture in your mind, realizing and knowing you have operated a definite, psychological law which is now working for you in the dark house of your mind. As you do this, you are truly watering the seed and fertilizing it; thereby accelerating its growth.

The conscious mind of man is the motor; the subconscious is the engine. You must start the motor, and the engine will do the work. The conscious mind is the dynamo that awakens the power of the subconscious.

The first step in conveying your clarified desire, idea, or image to the deeper mind is to relax, immobilize the attention, get still, and quiet. This quiet, relaxed, peaceful attitude of mind prevents extraneous matter and false ideas from interfering with your mental absorption of your ideal; furthermore in the quiet, passive, receptive attitude of mind effort is reduced to a minimum.

In the second step you begin to imagine the reality of that which you desire. For example you may wish to sell a home. In private consultation with real estate brokers I have told them of the way I sold my own home; they have applied it with remarkable results. I placed a sign in the garden in front of my home which read, "For sale by owner." The second day after placing the sign, I said to myself as I was going to sleep, "Supposing you sold the house, what would you do?"

I answered my own question, and I said, "I would take that sign down, and throw it in the garage." In my imagination I took hold of the sign, pulled it up from the ground, placed it on my shoulders, went to the garage, and threw it on the floor, saying jokingly to the sign, "I don't need you anymore!" I felt the inner satisfaction of it all, realizing it *was* finished. The next day a man gave me a deposit of $1,000, and said, "Take your sign down; we will go into escrow now."

Immediately I pulled the sign up, and took it into the garage. The outer action conformed to the inner. There is nothing new about this. "As within, so without," meaning according to the image impressed on the subconscious mind, so is it on the objective screen of your life.

This procedure or technique is older than our

Bible. The outside mirrors the inside. External action follows internal action.

I was engaged by a very large organization to do some spiritual work for them. Through fraudulent means others were trying to lay claim to their vast mining and other interests. They were harassing the company by legal trickery, and trying to get something for nothing. I told the lawyer to dramatize vividly in his imagination several times daily the president of the company which he represented congratulating him on the perfect, harmonious solution. As he sustained the mental picture, through continuous, mental application, the subjective wisdom gave him some new ideas,— as he said, "Right out of the blue!" He followed these up, and the case was closed soon afterwards.

If a person has a mortgage due at the bank, and he does not have the money to cover it, and if he will faithfully apply this principle, the subconscious mind will provide him with the money. Never mind how? when? where? or through what source? The subjective mind has ways you know not of; its ways are past finding out. It is one of the instruments or tools which God gave man, so he could provide himself with all things necessary for his welfare. The man who hasn't the money to meet the mortgage, can imagine himself depositing a check or currency required in the bank; i.e., giving it to the cashier. The important point is to become intensely interested in the mental picture or imaginary act, making it real and natural. The more earnestly he engages his mind on the imaginary drama, the more effectually will the imaginary act be deposited in the bank of the subconscious mind. You can take a trip to the teller's window in your imagination, and make it so real and true that it will actually take place physically.

There is a young lady who comes regularly to our Sunday morning lectures. She had to change busses three times; it took her one and one half hours each Sunday to come to the lectures. In the sermon I told how a young man prayed for a car and received one. She went home, and experimented as follows: Here is her letter in part published by her permission:

"Dear Dr. Murphy:

This is how I received a cadillac; I wanted one to come to the lectures on Sunday and Tuesdays. In my imagination I went through the identical process I would go through if I were actually driving a car. I went to the show room, and the salesman took me for a ride in one. I also drove it several blocks. I claimed the cadillac car as my own over and over again. I kept the mental picture of getting into the car, driving it, feeling the upholstery, etc., consistently for over two weeks. Last Sunday I drove to your meeting in a cadillac. My uncle in Inglewood passed away; left me his cadillac and his entire estate."

If you are saying now, I do not know of any way to get the money to pay off the mortgage; do not worry about it. *To worry* means to strangle. Realize there is a Power inherent within you which can provide you with everything you need when you call upon It. You can decree now with feeling and conviction, "My house is free from all debt, and wealth flows to me in avalanches of abundance." Do not question the manner in which the answer to your prayer will come. You will do the obvious things necessary knowing that the subconscious intelligence is directing all your steps; for it knows everything necessary for the fulfillment of your desires. You can imagine also a letter from the mortgage company informing you that you are paid up; rejoice in that image, and live with that imaginary letter in your mind until it becomes a conviction.

Become convinced now that there is a power within you capable of bringing what you imagine and feel as true into manifestation. Sitting idly

66

by, day dreaming, and imagining the things you would like to possess will not attract them to you. You must know and believe that you are operating a law of mind; become convinced of your God-given power to use your mind constructively to bring into manifestation the thing you desire.

Know what you want. The subconscious mind will carry out the idea, because you have a definite, clear-cut concept of what you wish to possess. Imagine clearly the fulfillment of your desire; then you are giving the subconscious something definite to act upon. The subconscious mind is the film upon which the picture is impressed. The subconscious develops the picture, and sends it back to you in a material, objectified form.

The camera is *you* consciously imagining the realization of your desire through focussed attention. As you do this in a relaxed, happy mood, the picture is cast on the sensitive film of the subconscious mind. You need also a time exposure; it may be two or three minutes or longer depending on your temperament, feeling, and understanding. The important thing to remember is that it is not so much the time as the quality of your consciousness, degree of feeling, or faith. Generally speaking the more focussed and absorbed your attention is, and the longer the time, the more perfect will be the answer to your prayer. *Believe that you have received, and ye shall receive.* "Whatsoever ye shall ask in prayer, believing, ye shall receive." *To believe* is to accept something as true, or to live in the state of being it; as you sustain this mood, you shall experience the joy of the answered prayer!

HOW TO IMAGINE SUCCESS

God is always successful in His undertakings. Man is equipped to succeed, because God is within him. All the attributes, qualities, and potencies of God are within.

You were born to win, to conquer, and to overcome! The Intelligence, Wisdom, and Power of God are within you waiting to be released, and enabling you to rise above all difficulties.

There are many men who quietly use the abstract term, "Success," over and over many times a day until they reach a conviction that success *is* theirs. Remember that the *idea of success* contains all the essential elements of success. As man repeats the word, "Success," to himself with faith and conviction, his subconscious mind will accept it as true of himself, and he will be under subjective compulsion to succeed.

We are compelled to express our subjective beliefs, impressions, and convictions. The ideal way to succeed is to know what you want to achieve. If you do not know your right place, or what you would like to do, you can ask for guidance on the question. The deeper mind will respond; as a result you will find a push or tendency in a certain field of activity.

The deeper mind is responsive to your thought. The subconscious—somtimes called "subjective or deeper mind"—sets in operation its unconscious intelligence which attracts to the individual the conditions necessary for his success. Man should make it a special point to do the thing he loves to do. When you are happy in your endeavor, you are a success.

Accept the fact that you have an inner Creative Power. Let this be a positive conviction. This Infinite Power is responsive and reactive to your thought. To know, understand, and apply this principle causes doubt, fear, and worry to gradually disappear.

If a man dwells on the thought, for example, of failure, the thought of failure attracts failure. The subconscious takes the thought of failure as his request, and proceeds to make it manifest in his experience, because he indulges in the mental practice of conceiving failure. The subconscious mind is impersonal and non-selective.

A business friend of mine, a tailor by trade, has

70

a favorite saying, "All I ever do is add. I never subtract." He means *success* is a plus sign. *Add* to your growth, wealth, power, knowledge, faith, and wisdom.

Life is addition! Death is subtraction. You add to your life by imagining whatsoever things are true, lovely, noble, and God-like. Imagine and feel yourself successful, and you must become successful. You are never a slave to circumstances, environment, or conditions. You are master of conditions. You can become a victim of conditions by mentally acquiescing to things as they are. As you change your mind, you change conditions.

A movie actor told me once that he had very little education, but he had a dream as a boy of being a successful movie actor. Out in the field mowing hay, or driving the cows home, or even when milking them, he said, "I would constantly imagine I saw my name in big lights in a large theatre. I kept this up for years until finally I ran away from home; got extra jobs in the motion picture field, and the day came when I saw my name in great, big lights, as I did when a boy!" Then he added, "I know the power of *sustained* imagination to bring success."

71

BELIEVE IN YOURSELF

What does *success* imply to you? You want undoubtedly to be successful in your relationship with others. You wish to be outstanding in your chosen work or profession. You wish to possess a beautiful home, and all the money you need to live comfortably and happily. You want to be successful in your prayers, and in your contact with the Universal Power within you.

Imagine yourself doing the thing you long to do, and possessing the things you long to possess. Become imaginative; mentally participate in the reality of the successful state; enter into that state of consciousness frequently; make a habit of it; then you will find you will be guided to do everything necessary for the realization of your dream. Go to sleep feeling successful every night and perfectly satisfied. You will succeed eventually in implanting the idea of success in your subconscious mind.

I know a drug clerk who was a licensed pharmacist receiving $40 a week plus his commission on sales. "After twenty five years," he told me, "I will get a pension and retire."

I said to him, "Why don't you own your own store? Get out of this place. Raise your sights! Have a dream for your children. Maybe your son wants to be a doctor; your daughter desires to be a musician."

His answer was that he had no money! He began to awaken to the fact that whatever he could conceive as true, he could give it conception.

The first step toward your goal is *the birth of the idea* in the mind, and the second step is the *manifestion of the idea.* He began to imagine he *was* in his own store. He participated in the act mentally. He arranged the bottles, dispensed prescriptions, imagined several clerks in the store waiting on customers. He visualized a big bank balance. Mentally he worked in that imaginary store. Like a good actor he lived the role. (Act as though I am, and I will be.) This drug store clerk put himself whole-heartedly into the act, living, moving, and acting in the assumption that his store was his.

The sequel was interesting. He was discharged from his position; went with a large chain store, became manager, and district manager. He made enough money in four years to make a down payment on a drug store of his own. He called it his "Dream Pharmacy." "It was," he said, "exactly the store he saw in his imagination." He became successful in his chosen field, and was happy doing what he loved to do.

The individual who habitually maintains a mental attitude of faith and expectancy of the best is bound to succeed and advance in life. The individual who is depressed, dejected, morbid, and despondent attracts failure all along the line. Fear is truly a lack of faith in Divine supply. It is faith misplaced. Fear is faith in the wrong thing. Fear is a belief in lack, or that man's good is being withheld from him.

"Son thou are ever with me, and all that I hath is thine." All things you need are in the invisible. It could be said, that all things needed are in the abstract. You must desire to be greater than you are, in order to advance in life. Desire comes first followed by a recognition of the Power within you enabling you to manifest what you want. The subconscious mind is the medium through which all that you desire can be brought into objectivity. You are the one giving orders in the form of habitual thinking, feeling, opinions, and beliefs. The subconscious mind obeys the orders given by the conscious mind. If your conscious mind is opposed to all negative thoughts, they can make no impression upon your subconscious mind. You become immunized.

If, for example, you say, "I wish I were healthy; then I could be much more successful in my work;" begin *now* to realize your body is your mind expressed. The subconscious mind is the builder of the body, and controls all its vital functions. Your conscious mind has power to change any idea or group of thoughts held in the subconscious mind. You can impress the idea of health on your subconscious mind when you know it can be done. A conviction and sincere belief is necessary. Affirmative statements establish definite impressions on the subsconscious mind.

A wonderful way to impress the subconscious is through disciplined or scientific imagination. By illustration if your knee is swollen, and you are lame, imagine you are doing the things you would do were you in perfect health. You might say that I would go down town on a bus, visit friends, ride horseback, go swimming, or hiking. First in your imagination you go on these psychological journeys, making them as real and natural as possible. *Continue* to go on these psychological journeys! You know that self-motivation is yours.

All movement is first of the mind or consciousness of man before any external movement can take place.

By example the chair does not move of itself. You must impart motion to it. The same is true of your body. As you continue to do all the things you would do were you healed, this inner movement will cause the subconscious to build the body in accordance with the image back of it.

The following is a wonderful prayer for perfect health. A minister I knew in South Africa applied this prayer, and healed himself. Several times a day he would affirm slowly and quietly, first making certain he was completely relaxed mentally and physically: "The perfection of God is now being expressed through me. The idea of health is now filling my subconscious mind. The image God has of me is a perfect image, and my subconscious mind recreates my body in perfect accordance to the perfect image held in the mind of God." This is a simple, easy way of conveying the idea of perfect health to your subconscious mind.

You can develop confidence by knowing and realizing that nothing can prevent you from achieving success. Develop a certainty in your mind that this Inner Power can be called upon to overcome all obstacles. There must be an assurance and determination on your part that you can achieve and accomplish what you set out to do. This positive, affirmative attitude constitutes confidence.

You have heard the Biblical expression, "According to your faith is it done unto you." Faith in God is the realization that there is only One Spiritual Power which is Omnipresent, Omniscient, Omnipotent, All Love, All Light, All Beauty, All Life, and An Ever-Present Help in time of trouble. Know that His Power responds to your thought.

Cease looking upon God as some Being living in the skies with a long beard. God is the Essence of man. God is the Life of man. We cannot comprehend all of God; for the finite mind cannot comprehend the Infinite en toto.

For example your conscious and subconscious mind are projections of God; they are working tools. God is Infinite Wisdom, Boundless Love, Infinite Intelligence, Absolute Bliss, Eternal Harmony, and Indescribable Beauty. All these, and others, are Qualities and Attributes of God.

BELIEVE IN YOURSELF

You are not cast adrift on the ocean of life deserted by the Creator of Life. This Presence and Power is within you. This Knowledge or Awareness of Divinity within you is the greatest and most powerful contributing factor to success.

Develop your talents; begin to use them; they are God-given. You have faculties and powers which require constant development.

"Man shall decree a thing, and it shall come to pass." What are you mentally decreeing now? What is the nature of your inner talking, inner conversation, and your idle moods? Man shall account for every idle word he speaks. The idle words are doubt, fear, anxiety, and worry. If these are present, you are not giving definite, positive orders to your subconscious mind, because there is no definite impression made as to what you wish to bring to pass.

Fear and worry cause confusion in the conscious mind. This creates confusion in the subconscious mind, and nothing happens but confusion in man's affairs. Continue to trust in the Divine Power, and that which you desire will come to you in some manner. Have faith in God, in the Divine Power, in His Divine Love, and His

Overshadowing Presence always watching over you, and you will become invincible. "Trust in the **LORD**, and do good; *so* shalt thou dwell in the land, and verily thou shalt be fed."

Made in the USA
Middletown, DE
10 August 2018